BOUGHT
with
BLOOD

Books by Derek Prince

Biography

Appointment in Jerusalem
Derek Prince: A Biography

Guides to the Life of Faith

Blessing or Curse: You Can Choose
The End of Life's Journey
Faith to Live By
God Is a Matchmaker
God's Remedy for Rejection
The Grace of Yielding
How to Fast Successfully
Husbands and Fathers
Marriage Covenant
Rediscovering God's Church
Rules of Engagement
Shaping History through Prayer and Fasting
Spiritual Warfare
They Shall Expel Demons
Through the Psalms with Derek Prince
Transformed for Life
War in Heaven

Systematic Bible Exposition

Entering the Presence of God
Foundational Truths for Christian Living
Lucifer Exposed
Promised Land
Self-Study Bible Course
You Shall Receive Power

BOUGHT

with

BLOOD

The Divine Exchange at the Cross

Derek
PRINCE

Chosen
Grand Rapids, Michigan

© 2000 by Derek Prince Ministries International

Published by Chosen Books
a division of Baker Publishing Group
P.O. Box 6287, Grand Rapids, MI 49516-6287
www.chosenbooks.com.

Previously published in 2000 under the title *Atonement, Your Appointment with God*

Printed in the United States of America

Library of Congress Cataloging-in-Publication Data
Prince, Derek.
    [Atonement, your appointment with God]
    Bought with blood : the divine exchange at the cross / Derek Prince.
       p. cm.
    Originally published : Atonement, your appointment with God. c2000.
    Includes index.
    ISBN 10: 0-8007-9424-9 (pbk.)
    ISBN 978-0-8007-9424-8 (pbk.)
    1. Atonement. I. Title.
BT265.3.P75 2007
232'.3—dc22
                                    2007006475

All royalties from this book are assigned to Derek Prince Ministries.

11   12   13   14   15   16   17   10   9   8   7   6   5   4

CONTENTS

INTRODUCTION

In the cross is health, in the cross is life,
in the cross is protection from enemies,
in the cross is heavenly sweetness,
in the cross strength of mind,
in the cross joy of the Spirit,
in the cross the height of virtue,
in the cross perfection of holiness.
There is no health of the soul, no hope of eternal life, save
in the cross.

> Thomas à Kempis, fifteenth-century theologian

In the closing years of his long and extraordinary life, Derek Prince lamented more than once what he saw as a decline in bold preaching focused on the cross. He saw Jesus' sacrifice as central to every aspect of the Christian life. In fact, to a group of ministry supporters and friends he once wrote:

> Anywhere I go, if I have the choice and opportunity to deal seriously with a group of people, it is my committed intention always to begin with the cross.
> And I would like to say to those of you who are preachers and ministers, do not ever leave the cross out of your

preaching. When you do, you're like the drill sergeant giving excellent orders to people without the power to carry them out. That power comes only from the cross.

In my preaching I remember the words of Paul in 1 Corinthians 2: "I determined not to know anything among you except Jesus Christ and Him crucified. . . . My speech and my preaching were not with persuasive words of human wisdom, but in demonstration of the Spirit and of power."

To explore Derek Prince's lifetime of teaching is nothing less than an exploration of the breathtaking depth and breadth of the redemption Jesus accomplished through His suffering, death and conquest of death. And nowhere will you find a better guide to that revelation than in the book you hold in your hands.

In *Bought with Blood* Derek brings us a complete and panoramic picture of what Jesus paid an awful price to obtain for us. On the pages that follow, you will find truths that have equipped hundreds of thousands to live more freely, more fully and more powerfully than ever before.

As Derek lays out the nine exchanges transacted at the cross, you will likely find that you have been living beneath your privileges as a blood-bought child of God. In the chapters covering the five aspects of deliverance, you will discover keys to a level of freedom you never dreamed possible. And as Derek shows you in the closing chapters how to appropriate these truths in practical terms, you will find greater access to the Holy Spirit's power for living the highest and best of God's will for your life.

Beyond all this, and perhaps most importantly, the journey on which Derek Prince takes you will surely produce in you a heart overflowing with love and thankfulness for Jesus. Such hearts belong to those used mightily by God!

The editors of Chosen Books

Part 1

THE CROSS
AT THE CENTER

1

ONE ALL-SUFFICIENT SACRIFICE

A single theme runs throughout this book: *atonement*. This word is comparatively rare in contemporary English. In fact, many English-speaking people today do not even know what the word means.

Its meaning begins to appear, however, when we divide the word up into its three syllables: *at-one-ment*. That is what *atonement* really means—that God and the sinner are brought into a relationship in which they are *at one*. A more common word today is *reconciliation*. Through the cross God and the sinner are *reconciled* to each other.

There is a vitally important difference between the word translated *atonement* in the Hebrew of the Old Testament and the word translated *atonement* in the Greek of the New Testament.

In Hebrew the word is *kippur* and means "covering." The Day of Atonement was a day of *covering*. By the sacrifices offered on that day, the sins of the people were *covered*—but only for one year. The next year at the same time, their sins had to be covered once more. The sacrifices offered that day provided no permanent solution, therefore, to the problem of sin; they merely provided a temporary covering. On each successive Day of Atonement, that covering was extended for one more year.

The picture of atonement in the New Testament is totally different. We see this when we contrast two passages in Hebrews—the book that deals, above all others, with Jesus as our High Priest and with the sacrifice He made on our behalf.

First, Hebrews 10:3–4 speaks of the sacrifices of the Old Testament: "In those sacrifices there is a reminder of sins every year." So, far from taking sin away, those sacrifices reminded the people of the problem of sin. "For it is not possible," the writer continues, "that the blood of bulls and goats could take away sins." The central issue here is *taking away* sins, not merely covering them.

In Hebrews 9:26, on the other hand, the writer speaks about what was accomplished by the death of Jesus, in direct contrast to the Old Testament sacrifices. In the second half of that verse, speaking of Jesus, the writer says: "But now, once at the end of the ages, He has appeared to put away sin by the sacrifice of Himself."

So when Jesus came and offered Himself as a sacrifice on the cross, He *put away* sin. This action contrasts with the Old Testament sacrifices, which merely reminded people of the fact that sin had not been dealt with and provided a covering that was valid for only one year.

When John the Baptist introduced Jesus in John 1:29, therefore, he said, "Behold! The Lamb of God who takes away the sin of the world!" Notice once again how different this is from the Old Testament. *Jesus took away sin.* For that reason, for those who have accepted His sacrifice, there remains no further sacrifice for sins.

What the Bible Says about Our Problem

Before I became a preacher (that was a long while ago now!), I was a professor of philosophy at Cambridge University in England. As a philosopher I decided one day to study the Bible. I considered it my philosophic duty to do so. Once I had read it through, I would be in a position, I felt, to pronounce my authoritative opinion on it. But while studying the Bible, I met the Lord in a dramatic, powerful and personal way. From that time until now there are two facts I have never doubted: first, that Jesus is alive; and second, that the Bible is a true, reliable and up-to-date book.

When I came to appreciate the Bible, I understood that what it offers is found in no other work of human wisdom or literature. In particular it reveals two matters of unique importance: the diagnosis of the human problem and the cure.

The Diagnosis: Sin

In the field of medicine, if a doctor cannot diagnose a condition, usually he cannot provide a cure. The diagnosis of the human problem, therefore, is of supreme importance. The Bible's diagnosis is given in one short word: *sin.* So far as I have been able to discover, no other book in the world, unless it derives from the Bible, diagnoses the problem of sin. Certainly no philosopher ever arrived at that diagnosis. It is unique to the Bible. If we had received nothing else from the Bible, we should be eternally grateful for the diagnosis of the human condition. But thank God, the Bible provides us not only with the diagnosis. It also reveals the remedy, which is *atonement*.

In this book we will consider the basic problem of humanity: *sin*. Not merely is it the fundamental problem of humanity in general; it is also the problem of each one of us individually, whether we recognize it or not. We may call it by various names. Some so-called sciences in the world today offer us lots of fancy, complicated names, but the root problem remains the same: sin. A person is unable to deal effectively with his or her life's problems until he or she has faced the reality of the root problem of life, which is sin.

The Bible's definition of sin is given in Romans 3:23: "All have sinned and fall short of the glory of God." The essence of sin is negative rather than positive. Sin is not necessarily committing some terrible crime. It is failing to give God His rightful place in our lives, leading lives that withhold from God the glory that all His creatures owe Him.

Once we understand the human condition in this way, we must acknowledge that what Paul says is true: We have all sinned, and we all fall short of the glory of God.

The Remedy: The Cross

Thank God, the Bible not only diagnoses our sin; it also provides God's perfect remedy, which is *the cross*.

When I speak about the cross, I am not referring to a piece of metal or wood that people hang around their necks or put up on the wall of a church, although I have nothing against such things. When I refer to the cross, I am talking about the sacrifice that Jesus made there on our behalf. The majority of Christians probably do not fully realize that what took place on the cross was a sacrifice. To substantiate this, we will look at three passages in Hebrews, all of which emphasize the cross as a sacrifice.

In Hebrews 7:27, speaking about Jesus and contrasting Him with the priests of the Old Testament, the writer says:

> [He] does not need daily, as those high priests, to offer up sacrifices, first for His own sins and then for the people's, for this He did once for all when He offered up Himself.

The word *offer* refers to what a priest did when he made a sacrifice. But on the cross Jesus offered up Himself. That is to say, He was both the Priest and the sacrifice. As Priest He offered the sacrifice, but He Himself was the sacrifice, the victim. He offered Himself. Only one Priest was good enough to make that offering, and only one offering would be acceptable to God.

Again in Hebrews 9:13–14 we see a direct contrast with the Old Testament:

> If the blood of bulls and goats and the ashes of a heifer, sprinkling the unclean, sanctifies for the purifying of the flesh, how much more shall the blood of Christ, who through the eternal Spirit offered Himself without spot to God, cleanse your conscience from dead works to serve the living God?

Notice that Jesus "*through the eternal Spirit* offered Himself without spot to God." This refers to the Holy Spirit, whose participation in the sacrifice was essential. We discover, in fact, that in every major phase of the process of redemption each Person of the Godhead is directly involved. Their involvement in each successive phase may be set out as follows:

1. *The Incarnation.* The Father incarnated the Son in the womb of Mary by the Holy Spirit (see Luke 1:35).
2. *Baptism in the Jordan River.* The Spirit descended on the Son, and the Father spoke His approval from heaven (see Matthew 3:14–17).
3. *Public ministry.* The Father anointed the Son with the Spirit (see Acts 10:38).
4. *The crucifixion.* Jesus offered Himself to the Father through the Spirit (see Hebrews 9:14).
5. *The resurrection.* The Father resurrected the Son by the Spirit (see Acts 2:32; Romans 1:4).
6. *Pentecost.* From the Father the Son received the Spirit, whom He then poured out on His disciples (see Acts 2:33).

Each Person of the Godhead—and I mean this reverently—was jealous to be included in the process of redeeming humanity.

But our present focus is on the cross, with Jesus, once again, as both Priest and victim. The Son offered Himself to the Father, through the eternal Spirit, without spot or blemish. He was totally pure—the only acceptable offering because He was the only One without sin.

Putting the Cross Back in the Center

The word *eternal* describes something that transcends the limits of time. What happened on the cross was a fact of history, but its significance transcends time. In that sacrifice Jesus took on Himself the sins of all people of all ages—past, present and future. Our limited human minds can hardly comprehend all that was accomplished through that one sacrifice. Your sin and my sin, and the sins of all who have ever lived, and of people not yet born, came on Jesus through the eternal Spirit. He took the entire sin of the whole human race on Himself.

It is extremely important that we understand this and that we give the cross its proper place in our thinking as Christians. Some years ago I was with a Christian co-worker in Singapore. In the course of conversation he remarked, "The Church has so many items in her shop window that the cross is no longer noticed."

I realized my friend had put his finger on a major defect in the contemporary Church. Today you can go into a Christian bookstore and find a book on almost any subject—how to have a better marriage, how to raise godly children, how to understand your own personality, how to keep a better house. There is almost no limit! Many of these books have merit, but none would be effective without the cross. The cross is the only source of grace and power to make all the other good advice work. It is time the Church put the cross back in the center of her shop window.

God told the Israelites before they entered the Promised Land that when they built an altar, they were to put no other objects around it.

In Exodus 20:24–25 God gave the Israelites specific instructions about the kind of altar on which they were to offer their sacrifices:

> "An altar of earth you shall make for Me. . . . And if you make Me an altar of stone, you shall not build it of hewn stone; for if you use your tool on it, you have profaned it."

Their altar was to be made only of materials in their natural condition, not modified in any way by man—earth or unhewn stone. Anything added by human hands would defile it.

Further on, in Deuteronomy 16:21, the Lord warned His people:

> "You shall not plant for yourself any tree, as a wooden image, near the altar which you build for yourself to the LORD your God."

There was to be nothing that would distract the attention of the Israelites from the altar on which they were to offer their sacrifices. There was no place for human art or ingenuity that would divert their attention from the crude, stark simplicity of the altar. That is a lesson for us, too. We are not to surround the cross with anything. We are to put nothing on the cross or in front of the cross that would in any way obscure it. The cross is stark, just as the crucifixion of Jesus was a stark and horrible scene.

I doubt whether any human artist has ever depicted adequately what took place when Jesus died on the cross. If he should succeed, we would avert our eyes. Yet the cross is at the center of our faith, unique to Christianity. No other religious system—not Islam nor Buddhism nor Hinduism nor any of the countless cults—possesses anything that corresponds to or even remotely resembles the cross.

Furthermore the cross anchors the Christian faith to history. Muhammad, by contrast, received his revelation in an unidentified cave, unconnected to any particular situation or series of events. In general, philosophers for their part speculate in the abstract. But the message of the cross relates to a specific incident in human history. It either did or did not happen. It is either true or false. There is no third possibility. If true it is the most important event in human history.

When I was confronted many decades ago with the central facts of the Gospel, and then discovered that Jesus was still alive in the twentieth century, I concluded that the fact that a Man died and rose from the dead and is still alive today is the most important single event in human history. Nothing else can compare with it.

If we do not give the cross its rightful place at the center of our lives, our faith loses its meaning and power. We end up with either an innocuous list of moral generalities or else a standard of conduct that we cannot attain to. No one will ever live out the Sermon on the Mount without the power of the cross in his or her life.

I have been praying for some years that God would enable the Church to restore the cross to its rightful place. I trust that this study on the atonement, and the divine exchange that took place as a result of it, may be part of the answer to that prayer.

What Are the Implications of the Cross?

Let's make a personal application. In 1 Corinthians 1:23 Paul says, "We preach Christ crucified." Let me ask you a question: If you are a preacher or teacher or counselor, or if you hold some other office in church, do you preach Christ crucified? If not, your preaching or teaching or counseling may sound nice, but in the long run it will accomplish nothing. The only source of the power is the cross.

Again Paul says in 1 Corinthians 1:25: "The foolishness of God is wiser than men, and the weakness of God is stronger than men." The cross is the foolishness and weakness of God. What could be more foolish than for God to permit His Son to be crucified by sinners? What could be weaker than the spectacle of a Man hung on a cross, His body lacerated and bleeding, dying in agony? But the weakness of God, Paul says, is stronger than men. The foolishness of God is wiser than men. The real source of strength and wisdom for the Christian lies in the cross. Without the cross we can have good morality, a host of good intentions and a lot of nice sermons, but we will have no significant results.

Consider Hebrews 10:14: "By one offering He has perfected forever those who are being sanctified."

He has perfected forever. The verb *has perfected* appears in the perfect tense. Only once was this sacrifice to be offered, never to be repeated—a perfect sacrifice that would completely perfect all who put their faith in it. What Jesus has done, and its effect in us, is perfect, complete, forever. Nothing can ever be taken from it. Nothing need ever be added to it. What God has done is complete, perfect, final. Never will it have to be changed or modified. But our appropriation of it is progressive. It is important to see this, especially as we continue to emphasize the perfection of the work.

You may be saying to yourself, *I don't have that kind of perfection or sanctification.* The truth is, none of us has it. I have studied and taught on this theme for more than fifty years, but I am still being sanctified. Our sanctification is progressive. We are those who are coming progressively closer to God, getting further and further separated from sin and the world, receiving more and more of God into our beings. That is what the revelation of the cross does for us and in us.

In the chapters that follow, I want to deal with three little-asked questions:

1. What does the cross do *for* us?
2. What must the cross do *in* us?
3. How do we appropriate practically what God has already done through the cross?

These questions are not often asked, but finding the answers to them will bring us to a deeper level of sanctification than we have ever known. The complete provision of God is always released through the sacrifice of Jesus on the cross. Attempting to find our provision any other way is bypassing the cross and is extremely dangerous. The study ahead will be somewhat lengthy and arduous, but it will reward you richly if you persevere.

Questions for the Study

1. In simple terms, what does *atonement* mean?
2. What modern word conveys the same meaning?
3. According to Hebrews 10:3–4, what can the sacrifices made on the Day of Atonement by the Jews not do?
4. According to Hebrews 9:26 and John 1:29, what does the sacrifice of Jesus accomplish?
5. After reading Romans 3:23, how would you define sin?
6. What is the remedy for sin?
7. Is Jesus' sacrifice on the cross centered in time or eternity?
8. The cross is the only source of what two things?
9. What truths have you learned from this chapter that affect you the most?

2

PERFECTED FOREVER

In the last chapter I explained that the death of Jesus on the cross was a sacrifice, and that as High Priest Jesus offered Himself as a sacrifice to God through the Holy Spirit. By that sacrifice of Himself He put away sin forever.

I also mentioned that I came to the Lord from a background in which I was not really familiar with the teaching of the Gospel or the truths of salvation. The Lord did not deal with me on an intellectual basis. He simply threw me into the deep end of the pool and said, "Swim!" I was baptized in the Holy Spirit before I knew there *was* a baptism in the Holy Spirit and before anyone could warn me against it. This led me to study the Bible. To my astonishment I discovered that the Bible is true, relevant and up to date. In fact, I had to look continually to Scripture for an explanation of the events that were taking place in my life.

All this was happening while I was serving in Britain as a soldier in the British Army in World War II. Shortly afterward my unit was sent to the Middle East, where I spent the next three years serving as a medical orderly (or hospital attendant) in the deserts of Egypt and Libya. I continued with my unit through the great battle of El Alamein, after which I developed a disease on my skin, particularly my feet and hands. Different doctors called the condition by a different name, each name longer than the previous one! None of the doctors, however, could heal the condition. Because I was unable to wear boots any longer, I had to be released from my unit. I spent the next full year in military hospitals in Egypt. I would not want to spend a year in a hospital anywhere, but a military hospital in Egypt would be very low on my list if I had a choice!

Week after week I lay in a hospital bed. I knew I was saved. I had received the Holy Spirit and had come to believe that the Bible really is true. That was as far as I had come. I had no other teaching. In a way God took over the job and taught me Himself. I lay in bed day after day saying to myself, *I know if I had faith, God would heal me.* The next thing I always said, however, was, *But I don't have faith.* I found myself in what John Bunyan in *The Pilgrim's Progress* called the Slough of Despond, the dark valley of despair.

I am relating all this because I want you to understand that the power of the cross is not merely a theory, nor is it the product of theology. It is a solid fact of experience. It works.

As I lay there in my gloom, a little book dropped into my hands entitled *Healing from Heaven.* It was written by a medical doctor named Lillian Yeomans who, suffering from an incurable illness, had become addicted to morphine. But through faith in the Lord and in the Bible, she was wonderfully delivered. She devoted the rest of her life to preaching and teaching on healing.

In this book appeared this sentence—actually, a direct quotation from the Bible—that transformed my life. It was from Romans 10:17: "Faith cometh by hearing, and hearing by the word of God" (KJV).

As I read this statement, a ray of brilliant light penetrated my gloom. I laid hold of two words: *faith cometh*. If you do not have faith, you can get it. How? By *hearing*. Hearing what? What God says in His Word.

I decided I would hear what God says. So I armed myself with a blue pencil and read through the entire Bible, underlining in blue everything that related to four themes: healing, health, physical strength and long life. It took me several months to do it—but, after all, I had nothing else to do! When I finished, do you know what I had? A blue Bible! The Scripture convinced me that God has provided healing through the sacrifice of Jesus Christ.

I still did not know, however, how to practically lay hold of healing.

A Word of Direction

In due course I was transferred to a hospital at Alballah on the Suez Canal. There I met a most unusual lady from Cairo. Mrs. Ross, a brigadier in the Salvation Army, had taken the rank of her husband at his death—the custom in the Salvation Army. Mrs. Ross was still more unusual because she was a tongues-speaking Salvationist, and there were not many of those in the 1940s. She was as militant about what she believed—speaking in tongues and divine healing—as Salvationists are about salvation. Mrs. Ross had been incurably sick with malaria twenty years earlier as a missionary to India. She had trusted the Bible and received complete healing from malaria, and had never taken another mouthful of medicine since.

Having been told of this Christian soldier in need of healing, Mrs. Ross took a rather difficult journey to visit me. She got hold of a little four-seater British car in Cairo and persuaded a New Zealand soldier to drive. These two, along with a young lady co-worker from Oklahoma, arrived at the hospital. Mrs. Ross marched into the ward in her Salvation Army uniform, complete with bonnet and cape, overawed the nurse and obtained permission for me to go out and sit in the car and pray with them. I was not even consulted!

I found myself in the back seat of that very small car, behind Mrs. Ross and the soldier and beside the sister from Oklahoma. We started to pray. After a few minutes the young American sister began, fluently and forcefully, to speak in tongues, and the power of God came down on her so that she was actually shaking physically. Then I found myself shaking, too. Then everybody in the car was shaking. Finally the car itself, though the engine was not running, was vibrating as though it were rumbling at fifty miles an hour over a rough road.

Somehow I knew God was doing this for my benefit.

Then the woman from Oklahoma gave the interpretation in English of her prayer in an unknown tongue.

Now, when you put a British professor of philosophy—a student of Shakespeare who appreciates Elizabethan English and the King James Bible—beside a young woman from Oklahoma, you are likely to have a clash of cultures and language. It astonished me, then, that this interpretation came in the most perfect Elizabethan English. I do not remember all that was said, but a certain passage is as fresh for me today as it was in 1943: "Consider the work of Calvary: a perfect work, perfect in every respect, perfect in every aspect."

You will agree, this is elegant English. I appreciated it immediately, especially with my background in Greek. The last words Jesus said on the cross were "It is finished." These words appear in the original Greek of the New Testament as a single word: *tetelestai.* This word, which occurs in the perfect tense, means "to do something perfectly." You could translate the word "perfectly perfect" or "completely complete."

Through the young woman from Oklahoma, the Lord was speaking to me of a perfect work, perfect in every respect, perfect in every aspect: *tetelestai.* I was overawed, because I knew the Holy Spirit was interpreting that word for me. God had spoken.

Yet I emerged from the car with the same skin condition. Nothing had happened physically. But I had received a word of direction from the Lord. What Jesus did for me on the cross contained all I would ever need for time and eternity—physically, spiritually, materially, emotionally.

Taking God's Word as Medicine

The work of the cross is "perfect in every respect, perfect in every aspect." It matters not from what point of view you look at the cross. It is perfect. Nothing has been omitted. "All things that pertain to life and godliness" (2 Peter 1:3)—and that covers just about everything!—are provided for in the sacrificial death of Jesus on the cross. Everything you will ever need, in time and eternity, whether spiritual or physical, financial or material, emotional or relational, has been provided by that one sacrifice. "He has perfected forever those who are being sanctified" (Hebrews 10:14). Notice again that word *perfected.*

So I set myself to understand what God did for me through Jesus on the cross. I began to see that on the cross Jesus bore not only my sins but also my sicknesses and pains, so that by His wounds I was healed. The message of Isaiah 53:4–5 was inescapable:

> Surely He has borne our griefs [literally, *sicknesses*] and carried our sorrows [literally, *pains*]; yet we esteemed Him stricken, smitten by God, and afflicted. But He was wounded for our transgressions, He was bruised for our iniquities; the chastisement for our peace was upon Him, and by His stripes [or wounds] we are healed.

My mind, trained to analyze, was able to see that there was no avoiding this conclusion: Jesus bore our sicknesses, our pains and our infirmities on the cross, and by His wounds we were healed.

I tried in every way, given my philosophical turn of mind, to set aside the implications of Isaiah 53:4–5. I considered every possible way to interpret it without including physical healing. In the next few weeks the devil brought to my mind probably every objection that has ever been raised against divine healing. I don't think he left out one! Yet every time when I went back to the Word of God, it said the same thing. I remembered my blue Bible. All the way through, starting in Genesis and ending in Revelation, I saw the promise of healing, health, physical strength and long life.

For some reason I had formed the conclusion that, as a Christian, you had to be prepared to be miserable for the rest of your life. Every time I read the promises and statements of healing in Scripture, I would say, "That's too good to be true. It couldn't really mean that. Could God really want me to be healthy, successful and long-lived? It couldn't be—that's not my picture of religion."

While I was arguing this way, the Lord spoke to me inaudibly but very clearly: *Tell Me, who is the teacher and who is the pupil?*

"Lord," I answered, "You're the teacher and I'm the pupil."

Well, would you mind letting Me teach you?

I got the message.

Then the Holy Spirit directed me to the Scripture that got me out of the hospital:

> My son, give attention to my words; incline your ear to my sayings. Do not let them depart from your eyes; keep them in the midst of your heart; for they are life to those who find them, and health to all their flesh.
>
> Proverbs 4:20–22

"My son . . ." I realized God was talking to *me* as His child. This passage is not addressed to unbelievers; it is addressed to God's people. When I came to the phrase *all their flesh*, I said, "That settles it!" Not even a philosopher could make *flesh* mean anything but flesh! "All my flesh" means my whole physical body. God has provided through His Word that which will impart health to my whole physical body.

I looked at the margin translation for *health* and it was "medicine," so the Hebrew word can be rendered either *health* or *medicine*.

This is wonderful! I said to myself. *I am sick and I need medicine. God has provided the medicine that will bring health to my whole body.*

One of my jobs as a medical orderly in the British Army was giving out medicine when I myself was not sick.

Now I said, "That's it. I'm going to take God's Word as medicine."

When I said this, God spoke to me again inaudibly but clearly: *When the doctor gives a person medicine, the directions for taking it are on the bottle. Proverbs 4:20–22 is My medicine bottle and the directions are on it. You had better study them.*

I went back and saw that there were four directions.

Number one: *Give attention to my words.* We must give undivided attention to what God is saying.

Number two: *Incline your ear.* We must bow those stiff necks of ours and become teachable. We do not know it all, and some of the traditions we have inherited from our church backgrounds are not biblical.

The third direction: *Do not let [my words] depart from your eyes.* We must keep our focus unwavering on the Word of God.

And finally: *Keep them in the midst of your heart.*

The next verse of Proverbs says this:

Keep your heart with all diligence, for out of it spring the issues of life.

Proverbs 4:23

Whatever you keep in your heart, in other words, will determine the course of your life. You cannot hold the wrong attitude in your heart and live right, nor can you have the right attitude in your heart and live wrong. The course of your life is determined by what fills your heart. God was saying to me, *If you will receive My Word through your ear gate, through your eye gate and admit it to your heart, it will do everything I have claimed.*

I made up my mind that I would take God's Word as my medicine. I went to the doctor and thanked him for trying to help me. "But from now on," I told him, "I'm going to trust God. I don't want any more medication."

I narrowly escaped being sent to a psychiatric hospital, and was discharged on my own responsibility.

Although the worst kind of climate for my skin condition was heat, the army sent me to a much hotter place, Khartoum in the Sudan, where the temperature regularly went up to 127 degrees. So there I found myself in the Sudan, struggling for healing but determined to take my medicine. Philosophically speaking it was a silly thing to do. Was I going to be clever and stay sick or silly and get healed? I decided to be silly.

So I asked myself, *How do people take regular medicine?* Often the answer was, three times daily after meals. So after each main meal I went aside by myself, opened up my Bible, bowed my head in prayer and said, "God, You have promised that these words of Yours will be medicine to all my flesh. I'm taking them as my medicine now in the name of Jesus." I would then read the Bible with careful attention and listen to what God was saying to me.

Thank God, I was perfectly healed! I received not merely physical healing, but I became a totally different person. The Bible renewed my mind and changed my priorities, values and attitudes.

Meeting the Conditions for God's Promises

It is wonderful to be healed by a miracle, and I thank God I have seen many people healed miraculously and instantaneously. There is real benefit, however, in being healed by "taking the medicine" systematically over time. You obtain more than physical healing; you are changed in your inner being.

I did not receive healing immediately. It took three months before I was fully healed in that difficult climate. In that situation I was encouraged by the example of the children of Israel in Egypt. The more the Egyptians afflicted them, the more the Israelites prospered and grew (see Exodus 1:12). Circumstances are not the decisive factor. God's promises do not depend on circumstances. They depend on *meeting the conditions.*

Let me close this chapter with a principle that will help you appropriate what you need from the sacrifice of Jesus. James said in his epistle that "faith without works is dead" (James 2:20). It is not sufficient just to sit and say, "I believe." You must activate your faith by appropriate deeds and actions.

The people who took me to my very first church service were friends of Smith Wigglesworth, the noted healing evangelist. He used to say, "Faith is an act." That is how it worked for me. I could have sat in bed and said, "I believe," but nothing would have changed. I needed to *do* something to activate my faith. In His wisdom God showed me to take the Bible three times daily as my medicine.

The lesson is clear: Do not be passive, but enter by the appropriate action into the provisions of the cross.

Questions for the Study

1. How does faith come?
2. What Greek word communicates the perfect work on the cross and what does it mean?
3. According to 2 Peter 1:3, how comprehensive is the provision made through the cross?

4. Are there areas in your life about which you argue with the Lord instead of letting Him teach you? What are they?

5. What lessons did you learn about coming to apprehend healing for yourself?

6. What are the four directions for taking God's Word as medicine?

7. Do God's promises depend on circumstances? On what, rather, do they depend?

3

A DIVINELY
ORDAINED EXCHANGE

In this chapter we glimpse an extraordinary truth: that through the sacrifice of Jesus on the cross an exchange took place that unlocks all the treasures of God's provision.

Let's begin our study of the divine exchange by reviewing Hebrews 10:14: "By one offering He has perfected forever those who are being sanctified." I have been emphasizing two things. First, the death of Jesus on the cross was a sacrifice ordained by God, in which Jesus as Priest offered Himself on behalf of the whole human race to God the Father. Second, I have been stressing that His was a perfect sacrifice. Nothing was omitted; nothing will ever have to be added. It is perfectly perfect, completely complete. Every need of every descendant of Adam has been totally provided for through that one sacrifice of Jesus on the cross.

It is important to grasp this fact. It is also important that we not let our attention wander from this sacrifice. We can get involved in many forms of teaching, ministry and Christian activity that may be good in their own way. But if they are separated from the sacrifice of the cross, ultimately they lose their effectiveness.

I will take a picture from the prophet Isaiah to illustrate a further point: The cross is the *center* of all God's provision. The whole Gospel *centers* on the cross. The prophet Isaiah illustrates this in a vivid way. Bear with me; it is worth the study!

The Cross Is at the Center

How many chapters are there in Isaiah? There are 66. How many books are in the Bible? The same, 66.

There are two major sections in Isaiah, chapters 1–39 and chapters 40–66 (or 27 chapters). Similarly there are 39 books in the Old Testament and 27 books in the New Testament. The latter 27 chapters of Isaiah have often been called the Gospel in the Old Testament.

These 27 chapters are divided, in turn, into three sets of nine chapters each: chapters 40–48, chapters 49–57 and chapters 58–66.

One feature of these three sets of nine chapters is very significant: Each one ends with an emphatic declaration that God will never compromise with sin. Turning to the last verse of Isaiah 48, we read, "'There is no peace,' says the Lord, 'for the wicked.'" Now turn to the last verse of chapter 57: "'There is no peace,' says my God, 'for the wicked.'" These two statements are almost identical.

Turning on to the last verse of chapter 66, we find: "They shall go forth and look upon the corpses of the men who have transgressed against Me. For their worm does not die, and their fire is not quenched. They shall be an abhorrence to all flesh." The words are not identical, but the truth is the same: Those who have transgressed and not repented will represent an eternal spectacle of the judgment of God.

Each of these three sections of nine chapters, then, ends with a similar declaration—that in spite of all His mercy, God will never compromise with sin that is not confessed and renounced.

The Central Message of the Central Chapter

The middle section of this part of the book of Isaiah is chapters 49–57. The middle chapter of this middle section is Isaiah 53, but the prophecy really begins in the last three verses of chapter 52:

Behold, My Servant shall deal prudently.

Isaiah 52:13

The word *behold* introduces the words *My Servant*—the title given to Jesus in this prophecy. You will probably need to look at your Bible in order to see this, but if you add the last three introductory verses of chapter 52 to the twelve verses of chapter 53, you get five sets of three verses:

1 Isaiah 52:13–15
2. Isaiah 53:1–3
3. Isaiah 53:4–6
4. Isaiah 53:7–9
5. Isaiah 53:10–12

You can see that the middle set of this middle chapter of the middle section of Isaiah is 53:4–6. I believe this is by divine appointment, because the truth it reveals lies at the absolute center and heart of the total message of the Gospel.

Consider what it says in the first two of these three verses:

> Surely He has borne our griefs and carried our sorrows; yet we esteemed Him stricken, smitten by God, and afflicted. But He was wounded for our transgressions, He was bruised for our iniquities; the chastisement for our peace was upon Him, and by His stripes we are healed.
>
> verses 4–5

One of the tragedies of the English translation of the Bible is that in this passage, the translators of the King James Version (which I consider a wonderful version) spiritualized words that are physical in their meaning. The translators say *griefs* and *sorrows* where the Hebrew actually says *sicknesses* and *pains*. The meaning of these two words for *sicknesses* and *pains* has been unchanged from the time of Moses to the present.

Also, the beginning of verse 4 says, "Surely He." The grammatical effect in Hebrew is to put the emphasis on the *He*, for two reasons. First, the word translated "surely" emphasizes the word that follows. Then again, Hebrew—like Latin and Greek and Russian and other languages, but not most European languages—does not need to insert the pronoun *He* because this meaning is present in the form of the verb itself. You put the pronoun in only if you want to emphasize it. Because the pronoun *is* put in here, the *He* is emphasized twice, first by the preceding word *surely* and then by the pronoun *He*.

Now we come to the crucial verse—the third verse of this middle set of the middle chapter of the middle section of the last part of Isaiah:

> All we like sheep have gone astray; we have turned, every one, to his own way; and the LORD has laid on Him the iniquity of us all.

Isaiah 53:6

What is the problem of the human race? What have we all done? Here is the diagnosis of the Bible. We have not all committed adultery, nor gotten drunk, nor stolen. But there is one thing each of us has done: We have turned to our own way, which is not God's way. God describes that as _iniquity._ The best modern equivalent, I think, is _rebellion._ The root problem of humanity is rebellion against God.

This human problem is universal. All of us, Jew or Gentile, Catholic or Protestant, Asian, American or African, without exception, have gone our own way. We are all in the same category; we are rebels.

But the marvelous message is, God has laid on Jesus the iniquity, the rebellion, of us all. One translation says God made to meet together in Him the iniquity of us all. All men of all races, all ages. Our iniquity, our rebellion, came on Jesus as He hung on the cross.

What Did Jesus Carry?

The word for _iniquity_ in Hebrew is _avon._ It is important to understand that it means not merely rebellion, but all the evil consequences of rebellion, the punishment of rebellion and all that rebellion brings on those who are guilty. Three passages from different parts of the Old Testament will convince you, I hope, that what I am saying is not some fancy interpretation but a direct application of the Bible.

First, listen to Cain after he heard God's sentence on the murder of his brother:

> Cain said to the LORD, "My punishment is greater than I can bear!"
>
> Genesis 4:13

The word for *punishment* here is *avon*. Cain's iniquity and the punishment of it were both included in one word. They were greater than he could bear.

Here is a second example. When Saul asked the witch of Endor to bring up Samuel for him in a séance, because the punishment for witchcraft was death, he also promised her:

> "As the LORD lives, no punishment shall come upon you for this thing."
>
> 1 Samuel 28:10

The Hebrew word, once again, is *avon*. Saul assured the witch that she would not be held guilty for her action and that punishment would not come upon her.

Third, we see the word *avon* twice in Lamentations 4. First in verse 6:

> The punishment of the iniquity of the daughter of my people.

There are two English words used here: *punishment* and *iniquity*. But in Hebrew there is only one word: *avon*. It can be translated *iniquity* or *the punishment of the iniquity*.

And in verse 22 of the same chapter:

The punishment of your iniquity is accomplished.

Again there is only one word in Hebrew, as you have guessed: *avon*.

So the word *avon* means rebellion, the punishment for rebellion and all the evil consequences of rebellion.

When we turn back to Isaiah 53, we understand that the Lord laid on the suffering Servant the rebellion of us all, the punishment of our rebellion and all the evil consequences of rebellion.

The Divine Exchange

This leads us to a fundamental truth—a key that, as I have said, unlocks all the treasures of God's provision. At the cross an exchange took place, divinely ordained and predicted by God. Very simple, but very profound. *All the evil due, by justice, to come to us came on Jesus, so that all the good due to Jesus, earned by His sinless obedience, might be made available to us.*

Now read through the nine specific aspects of the exchange listed below. If your circumstances permit, read them aloud with special emphasis on each of the opposites—punished or forgiven, wounded or healed, and so on.

1. Jesus was punished that we might be forgiven.
2. Jesus was wounded that we might be healed.
3. Jesus was made sin with our sinfulness that we might be made righteous with His righteousness.
4. Jesus died our death that we might share His life.

5. Jesus was made a curse that we might receive the blessing.
6. Jesus endured our poverty that we might share His abundance.
7. Jesus bore our shame that we might share His glory.
8. Jesus endured our rejection that we might enjoy His acceptance.
9. Our old man died in Jesus that the new man might live in us.

You will never be able to find any reason you deserved His exchange. It is the outworking of God's sovereign *grace*. It is the expression of His measureless *love*.

In addition to these nine vital exchanges that took place at the cross, there are five different aspects of deliverance that we may receive through the application of the cross in our lives. Through the cross we receive deliverance—

1. From this present evil age
2. From the law
3. From self
4. From the flesh
5. From the world

In the balance of this book we will study each of these exchanges and aspects of deliverance, and explain how you can appropriate all that God has provided through the atonement. The key word here is *grace*. Grace is something you can never earn or deserve. Most religious people do not enjoy God's grace because they are trying to earn it. But there is no way to earn what God did for you through the death of Jesus on the cross. There is only one way to receive it—by believing it. Stop trying to earn it. Quit trying to persuade yourself that you are almost good enough. You are not and you never will be! The only way you can receive the provision of Jesus on the cross is by faith.

Why did God send His own Son to the cross in our place? He did so because He loves us. Why does God love us? The Bible never offers an explanation, and eternity will be too short to find out. We do not deserve it, we did not earn it and there is nothing in us to warrant His incredible sacrifice. It was a sovereign choice of almighty God.

As we consider God's provision, it is important for us to understand two titles of Jesus. First, in 1 Corinthians 15:45:

> So it is written, "The first man Adam became a living being [or a living soul]." _The last Adam_ became a life-giving spirit.
>
> emphasis added

Many Christians call Jesus "the second Adam." But that is incorrect. Verse 45 calls Him the _last_ Adam. Does it make a difference? It does, as we will see in a minute.

But first we will go on to verse 47:

> The first man was of the earth, made of dust; _the second Man_ is the Lord from heaven.
>
> emphasis added

So Jesus is called first _the last Adam_ and then _the second Man_. We must get these titles right and in the right order. If we do not get them right, or if we put them in the wrong order, it does not make sense.

On the cross Jesus was the last Adam. He was not the last in the sense of time; there have been millions and millions of descendants of Adam born since then. But He was the last in the sense that the evil inheritance of the whole Adamic race came on him in its entirety as He hung on the cross. The total evil inheritance of our sin-cursed race came on Him. And when He was buried, it was all buried with Him. Our evil nature inherited from Adam was put away. Finished. Put out of sight.

Then, when Jesus arose from the dead, He arose as the second Man, a new kind of man, the beginning of the Emmanuel race, the God-man race. Everyone who is born again through faith in Jesus' death and resurrection becomes part of this new Emmanuel race. Make sure this is very clear to you. Picture Jesus on the cross, the last Adam, the end of it all. There was no other way for our race to escape the evil consequences of what we had done. But when Jesus was buried, it was all buried with Him. When He arose the third day, it was as the beginning of a new race, the God-man race, a race in which God and man are somehow mysteriously combined in one new creation.

In 1 Peter 1:3 the apostle compares the resurrection to a birth from the dead, and in Ephesians 1:22–23 Paul describes Jesus as "head over all things to the church, which is His body." That is a beautiful picture, because in a natural human birth, what part of the body emerges first? The head. The emerging head is the guarantee that the rest of the body will follow. When Jesus Christ, as Head of the Church, was resurrected from the dead, He became the guarantee of our resurrection. He died as the last Adam (extend your left hand), and arose as the second Man (now extend your right).

A Final Prophetic Picture

Now we will look at one final prophetic picture, a description of Israel's rebellion. In Isaiah 1:2 the Lord says about the sons of Israel:

"They have rebelled against Me."

In verses 5 and 6 the Lord gives a vivid picture of the consequences of this rebellion:

> The whole head is sick, and the whole heart faints. From the sole of the foot even to the head, there is no soundness in it, but wounds and bruises and putrefying sores; they have not been closed or bound up, or soothed with ointment.

That is rebellion and all its evil consequences. It is also an exact picture of Jesus on the cross! Compare this with part of the introduction to Isaiah 53:

> "See, my servant will act wisely; he will be raised and lifted up and highly exalted. . . . There were many who were appalled at him—his appearance was so disfigured beyond that of any man and his form marred beyond human likeness."
>
> Isaiah 52:13–14, NIV

Jesus' physical form was so marred that He lost the appearance of a human being. From the crown of His head to the soles of His feet were nothing but "wounds and bruises and putrefying sores."

Why was His appearance "disfigured beyond that of any man and his form marred beyond human likeness"? Because that is the outworking of rebellion. In one vivid picture God conveys to us the fact that, on the cross, Jesus bore our rebellion and all its evil consequences. Don't believe pretty religious pictures about the crucifixion. It consisted of wounds and bruises and putrefying sores. The wounds were open and they were septic. Why? Because the rebellion of us all was visited on Him. The next time you and I attempt to rebel, may God give us a picture of the end of rebellion. Jesus as the last Adam took that rebellion, died and was buried with it. When He rose again, He rose as the second Man, the head of a new race.

Say that aloud now, as you finish this chapter: "On the cross Jesus bore our rebellion and all its evil consequences." If you really believe what you just said, you have one more thing to say: "Thank You, Lord Jesus!"

Amen.

Questions for the Study

1. What is at the center of all God's provision and the Gospel?
2. What does Isaiah 53:6 identify as the problem of the human race?
3. How did God solve the problem of the human race?
4. What are the nine specific aspects of the divine exchange?
5. What are the five different aspects of deliverance that we receive?
6. What two titles of Jesus are important to understanding God's provision?
7. What is the significance of these two titles?

Part 2

THE NINE EXCHANGES

4

FORGIVENESS
AND HEALING

On the cross, as we have seen, a divinely ordained exchange took place—something conceived in the heart and mind of God from eternity and acted out at Calvary. The cross was no accident—not some grievous mishap forced on Jesus, not some development God had not foreseen. No, the cross was a marvel ordained by God from the beginning of time in which Jesus, as Priest, offered Himself to God as the sacrifice. By this one sacrifice He made provision for all the needs of the whole human race in every area of our lives, for time and for eternity.

The nature of the exchange was this: *All the evil due by justice to us came on Jesus, that all the good due to Jesus, because of His sinless obedience, might be made available to us.* Or, more briefly: *All the evil came on Jesus that all the good might be made available to us.*

In this chapter we will look at the first two aspects of this divine exchange, both of which are stated in Isaiah 53:4–5:

> Surely He has borne our griefs and carried our sorrows; yet we esteemed Him stricken, smitten by God, and afflicted. But He was wounded for our transgressions, He was bruised for our iniquities; the chastisement for our peace was upon Him, and by His stripes we are healed.

The First Exchange: His Punishment for Our Forgiveness

Isaiah explained, "The chastisement [or punishment] for our peace was upon Him." Here is the first exchange: *Jesus was punished that we might be forgiven.* As long as your sin is not forgiven, you cannot have peace with God. God will not make peace with sin.

It is significant, as we have noted, that each of the three nine-chapter sections in the second part of Isaiah ends with the statement that God will not compromise with sin. It has to be dealt with. The message of mercy is that sin was dealt with in Jesus on the cross. The wages of sin is death, but Jesus paid that penalty for us at Calvary.

And the result? Look at Romans 5:1:

> Therefore, having been justified by faith, we have peace with God through our Lord Jesus Christ.

Once our sin has been dealt with in God's way, the result is peace with God. If Jesus had not been punished, we could never have peace with God. As it is, His punishment made it possible for us to have peace.

We see this truth even more vividly in Colossians 1:19–22, which speaks about Jesus on the cross:

> It pleased the Father that in Him all the fullness [of God] should dwell, and by Him to reconcile all things to Himself, by Him, whether things on earth or things in heaven, having made peace through the blood of His cross. And you, who once were alienated and enemies in your mind by wicked works, yet now He has reconciled in the body of His flesh through death, to present you holy, and blameless, and above reproach in His sight.

That result could never be achieved any other way except by the sacrifice of Jesus. Because He became totally identified with everything evil that any man, woman or child ever did, it is possible for us to be forgiven and delivered from the power of evil.

Another Scripture on this theme is Ephesians 1:7:

> In [Jesus] we have redemption through His blood, the forgiveness of sins, according to the riches of His grace.

When we have forgiveness of sins, we have redemption. The word *redemption* means "to buy back" or "to ransom." Thus, through the price of the blood of Jesus given on our behalf as a sacrifice, we have been bought back from Satan to God.

In Romans 7, Paul gives a wonderful insight into this first exchange—an insight that is not clear to those unfamiliar with the cultural context.

When Paul says, "I am carnal, sold under sin" (verse 14), that phrase *sold under sin* relates to a Roman custom. When a person was being sold as a slave, he or she was made to stand on a block. From a post behind him, a spear was stretched out over his head. When you saw a person standing on the block under the outstretched spear, you knew that person was being sold as a slave. Paul was saying, in other words, "I am carnal, sold under the spear of my sin that is stretched out over my head. I have no options. I am here for sale."

Let's continue the comparison. When people were bought as slaves, they did not choose what they would do; the owner chose for them. Of two women sold in the same market, one might become a cook and the other a prostitute. They had no choice. That was true with us as sinners, as well. You may have been a "good, respectable" sinner and looked down on the prostitutes and addicts. But the slave owner still determined what role you as the slave would play, whether dignified or degrading.

The good news is this: One day Jesus walked into that slave market, selected you and said, "I will buy this person. Satan, you cannot have him [or her]. I have paid the price. From now on he [or she] is not your slave; he [or she] is My son [or daughter]." That is redemption! It comes only through forgiveness of sins. How can we be forgiven? Because Jesus was punished with the punishment due us.

The Second Exchange: His Wounding for Our Healing

Next we come to a truth that has been concealed from millions and millions of Christians: the physical aspect of the atonement. Here once again are the marvelous verses in Isaiah 53 that contain this physical aspect.

First:

> Surely He has borne our griefs [literally, *sicknesses*] and carried our sorrows [literally, *pains*].

verse 4

The second exchange, therefore, is this: *Jesus was wounded physically that we might be healed physically.*

The Hebrew uses two different verbs in this verse. When it says the suffering Servant "has borne our griefs," the Hebrew means He carried our sicknesses away. When it says He "carried our sorrows," the Hebrew means He endured our pains. Jesus has, therefore, carried our sicknesses away and has endured our pains.

What is the result? Look at the end of verse 5:

By His stripes [or *wounds*] we are healed.

How logical that is! Because Jesus has dealt with our sicknesses and pains in His own body, healing is provided for us. More literally the Hebrew says, "It was healed for us." Perhaps the best way to express this is, "Healing was obtained for us."

Isn't it interesting that when the Bible speaks about the atonement, it never puts healing in the future? It is finished! As far as God is concerned, healing has already been obtained. We are healed. Christians sometimes ask me, "How can I know if it is God's will to heal me?" I reply, "You've asked the wrong question. If you are a committed Christian sincerely seeking to serve God and do His will, your question should not be 'How do I know if it is God's will to heal me?' The question is, rather, 'How can I receive the healing God has already provided for me?'"

In future chapters I will try to deal, at least in part, with the question of how to appropriate what God has provided. If you do not believe that God has provided healing in the first place, however, you are not likely to appropriate it. The basis is discovering what God has provided through Jesus on the cross.

New Testament Reinforcements

You might say, "I'm not sure I accept your rendering of Isaiah 53." But you cannot argue with Matthew, Peter and the Holy Spirit. Both of these New Testament Jews, inspired by the Holy Spirit, quote Isaiah 53:4–5.

First let's look at Matthew 8:16 and the beginning of the public healing ministry of Jesus:

> When evening had come, they brought to Him many who were demon-possessed. And He cast out the spirits with a word, and healed all who were sick . . .

Note that in the healing ministry of Jesus, there is no hard and fast distinction between healing the sick and casting out evil spirits. All the way through His ministry, they go hand in hand. Why did Jesus minister like this? Verse 17 tells us:

> . . . that it might be fulfilled which was spoken by Isaiah the prophet, saying, "He Himself took our infirmities and bore our sicknesses."

Notice that the meaning of Isaiah 53:4–5, which Matthew is quoting, is totally physical, since he refers to *infirmities* and *sicknesses*. Furthermore its outworking is physical: Matthew says Jesus healed all who came to Him. Not some, but all. Every one! There is no question, then, that Matthew gives Isaiah 53:4–5 a totally physical application.

Just one more point from this Matthew passage. The emphasis in the phrase *He Himself* is on Jesus, not us. When you struggle with sin or sickness or depression or rejection or fear, the Bible says to look away from yourself. The answer is not in you. Turn your eyes to Jesus. "He Himself" is the answer.

A second New Testament passage also quotes Isaiah 53:4–5. It, too, speaks about Jesus,

> Who Himself bore our sins in His own body on the tree, that we, having died to sins, might live for righteousness—by whose stripes [again, *wounds*] you were healed.

> 1 Peter 2:24

Notice, again, that Peter's emphasis is on Jesus *Himself.*

Throughout these passages sin is the central issue. When sin is dealt with, everything else can be taken care of.

Finally notice the verb tense—not *will be healed,* not even *are healed,* but *were healed.* As far as God is concerned, it is already done. When Jesus said, "It is finished!" (John 19:30), it was finished. On God's side nothing will ever change it, nothing has to be added to it and nothing can be taken from it. Recall the prophetic word I received through the woman from Oklahoma before God gave me healing: "Consider the work of Calvary: a perfect work, perfect in every respect, perfect in every aspect." The physical aspect is just as perfect as any other.

What Does Salvation Include?

Let me now direct your attention to a number of passages in the New Testament in which the word for *save* is translated "heal" or "make well." The Greek word for *save* is *sozo.* All the other words for *salvation* are derived from the same root. In a significant number of passages in the New Testament, the verb *sozo* is used for physical healing.

The problem is, translators do not always translate the word "save," which obscures the fact that physical healing is part of salvation.

Healing Sōzō

We begin in Matthew 9:21–22, the story of the woman with the issue of blood who touched Jesus' garment and was then afraid to disclose what she had done. A woman with an issue of blood, you see, was considered unclean and was forbidden to touch anyone, since that person would then become unclean. So she transgressed by touching Jesus. This, rather than shyness, is why she came forward trembling when she was asked what she had done.

> She said to herself, "If only I may touch His garment, I shall be made well."
>
> Matthew 9:21

What she actually said was, "I shall be *saved*."

> But Jesus turned around, and when He saw her He said, "Be of good cheer, daughter; your faith has made you well."
>
> verse 22

He actually said, "Your faith has *saved* you."

Luke 8:47–48 gives us a further insight concerning the woman with the issue of blood:

> When the woman saw that she was not hidden, she came trembling; and falling down before Him, she declared to Him in the presence of all the people the reason she had touched Him and how she was healed immediately.

Once again, the word translated "healed" is really *sozo*, or "saved."

Jesus' response to her, "Your faith has made you well," is really "Your faith has saved you." Jesus, you see, includes healing as part of our salvation.

Now look at Mark 6:56:

> Wherever [Jesus] entered, into villages, cities, or the country, they laid the sick in the marketplaces, and begged Him that they might just touch the hem of His garment. And as many as touched Him were made well.

Once again the Greek word for "made well" is *sozo*, meaning "saved." What were they saved from? Once again, the answer is *from sickness*.

Deliverance from Demons

In Luke 8:35–36 we have the record of the man with the legion of demons. When Jesus cast the demons out, he became perfectly normal.

> Then [the people] went out to see what had happened, and came to Jesus, and found the man from whom the demons had departed, sitting at the feet of Jesus, clothed and in his right mind. And they were afraid. They also who had seen it told them by what means he who had been demon-possessed was healed.

Once again the Greek word used is *sozo*, which means "saved," this time translated as "healed." Deliverance from demons has been provided by the sacrifice of Jesus on the cross and is part of salvation.

I have ministered to thousands who needed deliverance from evil spirits, and have learned by experience that Satan respects only one thing: the cross. You can tell him you are a Baptist or an Episcopalian or a Presbyterian or a Pentecostal, and he could not care less. When you come against him on the basis of what Jesus did on the cross, however, Satan trembles.

Resurrection from the Dead

We move on to Luke 8:49–50:

> While [Jesus] was still speaking, someone came from the ruler of the synagogue's house, saying to him, "Your daughter is dead. Do not trouble the Teacher." But when Jesus heard it, He answered him, saying, "Do not be afraid; only believe, and she will be made well."

Again, as you realize by now, the Greek word behind "made well" is *saved*. "Salvation" here is being brought back from the dead.

Appropriating Salvation

So we see that physical healing, deliverance from evil spirits, even a little girl being raised from the dead, are all described by that one inclusive word *to save*. Salvation is everything provided by the death of Jesus on the cross.

In Acts 4:7 the apostles were questioned as to how they healed the lame man at the Beautiful Gate.

> Then Peter, filled with the Holy Spirit, said to them, "Rulers of the people and elders of Israel: If we this day are judged for a good deed done to a helpless man, by what

means he has been made well [or *saved*], let it be known to you all, and to all the people of Israel, that by the name of Jesus Christ of Nazareth, whom you crucified, whom God raised from the dead, by Him this man stands here before you whole."

verses 8–10

What produced wholeness in the lame man? Salvation. Then Peter drives home the point:

"Nor is there salvation in any other."

verse 12

Finally we turn to 2 Timothy 4:18:

The Lord will deliver me from every evil work and preserve me for His heavenly kingdom.

Where the translation says *preserve*, Paul used the word *sozo*. He was affirming, "The Lord will save me and keep on saving me."

The ongoing outworking of what Jesus did for us on the cross is salvation. From the moment you believe until the moment you pass out of time into eternity, you are moving in salvation provided by the sacrifice of Jesus on the cross.

Here, then, is an appropriate challenge:

How shall we escape if we neglect so great a salvation?

Hebrews 2:3

There are people who actually refuse salvation. They turn it down because they neither want it nor believe it. But multitudes of professing Christians do not refuse salvation; rather, they neglect it. They do not find out what God has provided for them but accept some traditional view, some denominational presentation of the cross.

God drove me to the place, through extended illness, where I had to find out what was included in salvation. I had no other way out. Perhaps God has brought you to that place, too. You cannot afford to neglect His salvation. Somewhere down the road—and even right now, perhaps—you need it desperately.

May God help each of us not to neglect the physical aspect of His great salvation.

Claiming These Exchanges

One of the simplest and most practical ways to appropriate what God has done is to thank Him for it, *confessing* it with your mouth. I will, therefore, put these first two exchanges in the form of verbal confessions:

Jesus was punished that I might be forgiven.

Jesus was wounded that I might be healed.

If you really believe these statements, you are bound to say, "Thank You, Jesus, for bringing me, through Your sacrifice, forgiveness and healing!"

Questions for the Study

1. What, in a single statement, is the nature of the exchange on the cross?

2. What stands in the way of our having peace with God?
3. What does the word *redemption* mean?
4. How can we be forgiven?
5. According to Isaiah 53:5, when can we be healed and why?
6. What does salvation include?
7. According to Hebrews 2:3, what must we be sure not to do?
8. Confess with your mouth the two exchanges given at the end of the chapter.

5

RIGHTEOUSNESS IN PLACE OF SIN

In this chapter we will look at Satan's attempts to make Christians feel guilty, and how we can overcome our accuser. Our victory is based on the third aspect of the divine exchange accomplished by Christ's perfect work on the cross: the exchange of sin for righteousness. This is another truth that many of us professing Christians have failed to grasp, so that we have been robbed of part of our spiritual inheritance.

First, however, we must distinguish between *sins* (plural) and *sin* (singular). *Sins* are the sinful acts we have committed. Jesus was punished that those sinful acts might be forgiven. *Sin* is the evil power, or evil nature, that causes us to commit sins. Until that evil power of sin has been dealt with, our deliverance is not complete.

So we turn again to the great atonement chapter, Isaiah 53.

It pleased the LORD to bruise Him; He has put Him to grief. When You make His soul an offering for sin, He shall see His seed, He shall prolong His days, and the pleasure of the LORD shall prosper in His hand.

verse 10

What a clear prediction of the resurrection of Jesus! After He had been made "an offering for sin," Scripture says the suffering Servant would "see His seed, He shall prolong His days, and the pleasure of the LORD shall prosper in His hand." This could not happen if Jesus remained dead!

But let's focus on the statement that God the Father made the soul of Jesus the sin (or guilt) offering. The key word here is *guilt*. We must always bear in mind that the sacrifices of the Old Covenant were just a preview of what God was going to do through the sacrifice of Jesus.

Under the Old Covenant, if a person committed a certain type of sin, he was required to find the appropriate offering. The person would bring that sacrifice, whether a bull or goat or sheep, to the priest at the Tabernacle and confess his sin. Then he would lay his hand on the head of the sacrificial animal and, by that act, symbolically transfer the sin from himself to the animal. Once the sin had been transferred, he would exact the penalty from the animal, and not from himself, by killing the animal. The animal was, in a sense, paying the penalty for the person's sin.

All this is a picture of what happened when Jesus was nailed to the cross. God the Father transferred all the sin of humanity to the soul of His Son. Isaiah makes an amazing statement that none of us will ever fully fathom: "You make His soul an offering for sin." Jesus' soul was made the sin offering for the entire human race!

When we consider the absolute purity and holiness of Jesus, we cannot even begin to comprehend what was involved in making His soul the sin offering for humanity. All of us can think of things we wish had never happened or that we had never done. We all feel a sense of embarrassment, perhaps even revulsion, at certain memories. Now think of the sinless Son of God taking on Himself the total sinfulness of the entire race! This was the cup He was reluctant to drink in Gethsemane. As Christ viewed both the physical suffering and the awful spiritual burden of human sin that He was going to take on Himself, He said, "Father, if it is Your will, take this cup away from Me" (Luke 22:42). Thank God He added, "Nevertheless not My will, but Yours, be done." Thus was our atonement purchased!

Now we need to turn to the New Testament. Perhaps you have read 2 Corinthians 5:21 without realizing it is actually quoting Isaiah 53:10:

> [God] made Him who knew no sin [that is, Jesus] to be sin for us, that we might become the righteousness of God in Him.

What is the opposite of sinfulness? In a word, righteousness. Here, then, is the exchange: *Jesus was made sin with our sinfulness, that we might be made righteous with His righteousness.*

This is a staggering thought! But it is utterly scriptural. We will never attain the righteousness of God by simply trying to be good. There is only one way for us to apprehend the righteousness of God: *by faith*. We have to believe the unbelievable: that Jesus was made sin with our sinfulness that we might become the righteousness of God in Him. What a breathtaking revelation!

Not Only Saved, but Justified!

Another passage in the book of Isaiah reveals a beautiful picture of this exchange and its results:

> I will greatly rejoice in the LORD, my soul shall be joyful in my God; for He has clothed me with the garments of salvation, He has covered me with the robe of righteousness.
>
> Isaiah 61:10

The writer does not say, "I will be moderately happy," but, "I will greatly rejoice." The word for *rejoice* in Hebrew is *sous*; when you want to be really emphatic, you repeat the verb: *sous asees*, I will "rejoice rejoicing" in the Lord. Why? Because there has been a double transaction.

First, God has taken away the filthy garments of our sin and clothed us with the garments of salvation. It is wonderful to be clothed with the garment of salvation. But don't stop there! God also wants to cover us with the robe of righteousness. One of the modern versions says, "He has wrapped me around with a robe of righteousness." You can be not only saved from sin but also clothed with the righteousness of God in Jesus Christ.

The technical word for this is *justified*. In biblical language *justified* and *righteous* are from the same root. *Justified* means "made righteous" or "made just." *just as though I've never sinned*

Let's suppose you are being tried in the Supreme Court of the universe for a crime that carries the mandatory penalty of death. You sit awaiting the verdict, and it finally comes back: *Not guilty.*

Believe me, you would be excited! You would not stroll to the front of the courtroom, shake the judge by the hand and say, "Thank you, Judge, that was a nice message." Nor would you tell your spouse and friends, "We had a good session this morning." You would hug your spouse, clap your friends on the back, jump up and down and shout, "I'm not guilty! I'm acquitted! I'm free!" An intolerable burden would have rolled off your shoulders.

This is what it means to be justified. My case has been tried in the Supreme Court of heaven and the court has handed down the verdict: *Not guilty*. I am acquitted, not guilty, made righteous, justified, "just-as-if-I'd" never sinned! There is nothing on which the devil can put his finger and say I am guilty.

When I regularly attended an Anglican church as a youth in Britain, it did not seem to my critical teenage mind that the people who recited the lovely words from the prayer book really believed what they were saying. I had a mental picture of one of those dignified ladies walking out of church and dropping her lace handkerchief. I would run up behind her and say, "Madam, here's your handkerchief. You dropped it." I pictured her more excited about getting her handkerchief back than about all the things she had said in church! Why? Because what she said and heard *had not been made real to her.*

I am trying to make real to *you* the fact that you are justified. Nothing in the record of heaven appears against you. If you keep your position in Christ, there is nothing Satan can accuse you of.

Guarding against Guilt

Satan's primary weapon against humanity is guilt. Be very careful about anyone or anything that makes you feel guilty; it does not come from God. The Holy Spirit "[convicts] the world of sin, and of righteousness, and of judgment" (John 16:8)—but that is different from guilt.

When the Holy Spirit convicts of sin, He says, "You did this. It was wrong. You need to repent and put it right. This is how you do that." Once you have confessed and repented and done whatever is necessary to make restitution, the matter is closed. There are no afterthoughts, nothing further that you should or should not have done.

With guilt, however, you never quite know if you have done enough. Perhaps someone feels you did not treat him or her right and is feeling rejected, upset and hurt. Yet somehow it does not matter what you say or do to that person; it is never enough. That is not the Holy Spirit working; that is another, evil power, from a different source.

Be on your guard, then, against anything that makes you feel guilty. This is a denial of the work of the cross—very different from the specific conviction of the Holy Spirit. Guilt never ends; it goes on and on. Nothing you can do is ever sufficient. If Satan persists in his attempts to make you feel guilty, you can take your stand on God's promise in Isaiah 54:17:

> "No weapon formed against you shall prosper, and every tongue which rises against you in judgment you shall condemn. This is the heritage [or *inheritance*] of the servants of the LORD, and their righteousness is from Me," says the LORD.

What wonderful news! Nothing the devil devises as a weapon against you will succeed! So relax. He may continue to use the weapon of guilt against you, but he will ultimately fail.

Notice, too, that God does not say *He* will condemn every tongue that rises against you; He says *you* will do that. On the basis of what Jesus has done for you on the cross, you must reject all Satan's accusations and refuse to come under guilt and condemnation. It is not your righteousness, after all, that is being challenged, but God's righteousness transferred to you. On that basis you can reject every accusation against you. You are not guilty. Remember that robe of righteousness! It does not matter from what angle the devil approaches you. All he can see is the righteousness of Christ covering you. This is summed up in Romans 8:1:

> There is therefore now no condemnation to those who are in Christ Jesus.

Romans 8 is the picture of the Spirit-controlled life. Verse 1 is the entrance to that life, and it is marked *No condemnation*. You cannot live the Spirit-controlled life while under condemnation, so you must learn to deal with condemnation. God says that you must condemn *it*! Why? Because Jesus was made sin with our sinfulness, that we might be made righteous with His righteousness.

Revelation 12:10 paints a picture of the final conflict of the ages between the people of God and the kingdom of Satan:

> Then I heard a loud voice saying in heaven, "Now salvation, and strength, and the kingdom of our God, and the power of His Christ have come, for the accuser of our brethren, who accused them before our God day and night, has been cast down."

What an incredible picture of events that I believe to be still in the future—a picture of continual accusation before the throne of God. Satan is accusing us constantly before the throne of God, trying to prove us guilty. How do we overcome our accuser?

"[God's people] overcame him by the blood of the Lamb and by the word of their testimony."

verse 11

When we testify personally to what God's Word says that the blood of Jesus does for us, and to what God has done, Satan has no answer.

Confessing the Exchange

One of the simplest and most practical ways to appropriate what God has done, as I pointed out in the last chapter, is to thank Him for it, confessing it with your mouth. Once again, then, claim this third exchange in the form of a verbal confession:

Jesus was made sin with my sinfulness that I might be made righteous with His righteousness.

Thank You, Jesus, for making me righteous!

Questions for the Study

1. What is the difference between *sins* and *sin*?
2. What is the opposite of sinfulness?
3. How do we apprehend righteousness?
4. What does it mean to be justified?
5. What is Satan's primary weapon against humanity?
6. What is the basis for our rejection of all Satan's accusations, guilt and condemnation?
7. Confess with your mouth the exchange given at the end of the chapter.

6

LIFE IN PLACE OF DEATH

So far we have covered three vital aspects of the divinely ordained exchange that took place when Jesus died on the cross:

Jesus was punished that I might be forgiven.

Jesus was wounded that I might be healed.

Jesus was made sin with my sinfulness that I might be made righteous with His righteousness.

Now we turn to the fourth aspect of the exchange, which is simple yet powerful: *Jesus died our death that we might share His life.*

It cost Jesus His life to make life available to us. He said in John 10:10: "The thief does not come except to steal, and to kill, and to destroy. I have come that they may have life, and that they may have it more abundantly."

There is an enormous difference between what Jesus gives us and what we deserve: "The wages of sin is death, but the gift of God is eternal life in Christ Jesus our Lord" (Romans 6:23). Here is a deliberate contrast between wages and a free gift. Wages are what we have earned for what we have done. Receiving them is justice; anyone who withholds your wages is unjust. But the free gift is something you cannot earn. You would be foolish, therefore, to say, "All I want is justice." If you want justice, God, who is absolutely just, will give it to you. Justice demands that you receive your wages—and your wages are death.

Loren Cunningham related the story of a woman who went to a portrait studio and had her photograph taken. Later, when she went back to look at the proofs, she did not like what she saw. "These pictures don't do me justice!" she exclaimed to the photographer. He looked at her and said, "Madam, you don't need justice; you need mercy!"

I have thought about this story ever since. And I say to myself from time to time, *I don't need justice; I need mercy.*

Mercy is the alternative to justice. If you decline your wages, you qualify to receive the free, unearned gift of eternal life. It is available because Jesus accepted the wages of sin that were due to us, receiving them in our place, as Hebrews 2:9 states that Jesus "was made a little lower than the angels, . . . that He, by the grace of God, might taste death for everyone." He tasted death for you and for me!

Recall from chapter 3 that Jesus, who tasted death on behalf of every descendant of Adam, was "the last Adam" (1 Corinthians 15:45) and "the second Man" (1 Corinthians 15:47). As the last Adam, He terminated the whole evil inheritance that was due Adam and all his descendants, including you and me. When Jesus died, He said, "It is finished." That was the end. When He was buried, that evil inheritance was buried with Him. He rose again on the third day as the second Man, the head of a new race. Jesus died our death that we might share His life.

We need to look back into the Old Covenant to understand precisely the nature of this exchange.

God's Overpayment for Our Redemption

I would like to develop a concept that, if you can grasp it, will help you appropriate more of the life of God and make Jesus even more precious to you. For this purpose we need to search out certain words in Scripture that are translated by the English word *life*. We turn to the principles of divine justice laid down in the law of Moses.

One Soul for Another

Exodus 21:23–25 deals with wrongful injury of another person: "If any harm follows, then you shall give life for life, eye for eye, tooth for tooth, hand for hand, foot for foot, burn for burn, wound for wound, stripe for stripe." Something of equal value must be given to replace what was destroyed.

Translations sometimes obscure the meaning of words, both in the Old Testament and in the New. In fact, in this case a great and basic revelation of the Old Testament has been obscured by translation. Let's look at the implications of the word *life* in the first phrase, *You shall give life for life*.

The Greek of the New Testament contains three completely different words, all of which are translated into English in most versions as "life": *psuche*, which is soul; *zoe*, which is eternal life; and *bios*, which is natural life. In the Old Testament Hebrew there is a very interesting word—*nefesh*, which means primarily "soul," "life" or "person." When Genesis 2:7 says that "man became a living being," it uses the Hebrew word *nefesh*. Out of the union of the Spirit of God and clay emerged something totally new—Adam, a person, a new life, a new personality, a *nefesh*.

When Exodus 21:23–25 refers to giving "life for life," the Hebrew is "*nefesh* for *nefesh*"—soul for soul. If one person is killed in a crime, for example, the other soul has to pay the penalty with his life.

Compare this passage with Deuteronomy 19:21: "Your eye shall not pity: life shall be for life." The same principle: *nefesh* in place of *nefesh*, one soul in place of another soul.

The Soul Is in the Blood

What *is* the soul? Leviticus 17:11 contains the answer, as God speaks in a marvelous prophetic Scripture:

> "The life of the flesh is in the blood, and I have given it to you upon the altar to make atonement for your souls; for it is the blood that makes atonement for the soul."

In the opening phrase *the life of the flesh*, the Hebrew word for *life*, once again, is *nefesh*. The "soul" of the flesh is in the blood.

What is the significance of this? Man possesses spirit and soul and body. When the spirit leaves, he ceases breathing. When the soul leaves, his blood no longer flows. The soul of the flesh is in the blood. And so God says, "I have given it—the soul, or the life—to you on the altar to make atonement for your souls." In other words, one soul has to make atonement for another soul. Since the soul resides in the blood, blood must be shed in an atonement—the giving of one life for another.

Now we return to the great atonement chapter, Isaiah 53. In the closing verse of the chapter, ending the section about what the Servant of the Lord has accomplished in His sufferings, we read these words:

> I will divide Him a portion with the great, and He shall divide the spoil with the strong, because He poured out His soul unto death, and He was numbered with the transgressors, and He bore the sin of many, and made intercession for the transgressors.

Some translations use the word *life* instead of *soul*: "He poured out His life unto death." But the Hebrew word is *nefesh*. *Soul* is the better translation. How did Jesus pour out His soul to death? Through His blood. His soul was given on behalf of all humanity as Jesus bled and died on the cross.

Personally, as I read the account of the crucifixion, I form the impression that Jesus' body was virtually emptied of blood. They lacerated His back. They pressed thorns into His head. They pierced His hands and feet. He was bleeding profusely. Then, after He had actually expired, a soldier thrust a spear into His heart, and out came water and blood. It was as if all the blood of His body was poured out on the cross. This was His offering of His soul, as the last Adam, on behalf of all the Adamic race.

Appreciating the Blood of Jesus

As a logician by background, I can accept doctrines by faith and believe them, but sooner or later I want them to make sense logically. It was only when I began to meditate on the truth about the soul being in the blood that this concept became vivid and logical to me.

For years I had believed in the atonement—that Jesus was the offering for sin. I knew His offering provided forgiveness for all humanity. But then I began to meditate on *how* the soul of the Son of God was given on behalf of humanity. I considered that the life of God the Creator is infinitely more valuable than the life of all the creatures He has ever created. The soul of the Son of God was more than sufficient atonement for all the souls of the whole human race. Psalm 130:7 says, "With Him is abundant redemption." In other words, God not only paid, but He overpaid for our redemption!

This is the concept that, if you can grasp it, will make Jesus infinitely more precious to you. His one soul, which He gave on the cross through His blood, was the offering to redeem the whole human race, on the principle we have just examined: a soul for a soul.

We must be very, very careful, then, about how we speak of the blood of Jesus. I have heard even evangelical and charismatic ministers say, "The blood was 'negative'; it simply paid the price of sin."

I don't believe that, and I advise you never to entertain any such thinking or to devalue the blood of Jesus. Unfortunately the Church today is permeated with all sorts of unscriptural teachings. Some denominations have even removed from their hymnbooks every reference to the blood of Jesus. Who is behind that? Certainly not God!

As Leviticus 17:11 says, "The life . . . is in the blood." Life is not negative, is it? Life is the most positive thing you can ever encounter. The life of God is in the blood of Jesus; and the whole of heaven views with abhorrence anything that downgrades the blood of Jesus, because all heaven was witness to the sacrifice in which Jesus poured out every drop of His life blood.

Furthermore I believe that when we express our appreciation for the blood of Jesus, we attract the Holy Spirit. Recall the beautiful hymn of Charles Wesley, "Arise, My Soul, Arise!" containing the line, "His Spirit answers to the blood." When we proclaim the truth about the blood of Jesus, the Holy Spirit says, "That is where I want to be. Those people are saying things I like to hear."

Feeding on Jesus' Blood

In John 6:54–56 Jesus said:

"Whoever eats My flesh and drinks My blood has eternal life, and I will raise him up at the last day. For My flesh is food indeed, and My blood is drink indeed. He who eats My flesh and drinks My blood abides in Me, and I in him."

This concept offended some of Jesus' disciples to the point that they did not follow Him any longer. It still antagonizes people today. After all, there is something rather offensive about blood. Whenever I think of blood, my stomach begins to turn over. When I was a small boy I could not look at blood without actually vomiting. It took me years to get over that revulsion. Something in every one of us does not like the thought or spectacle of blood.

Some things that are offensive, however, are necessary. The cross is an offense, but without it there is no redemption, no hope. Our hope depends entirely on the merits of the blood of Jesus.

Then Jesus said to them, "Most assuredly, I say to you, unless you eat the flesh of the Son of Man and drink His blood, you have no life in you."

John 6:53

Why? Because the life is in the blood.

For us to have life, we must feed on Jesus. We must appropriate what is in His blood.

The only Person in the universe who has life within Himself is God. None of us has life in ourselves since none of us has the origin of life within us. Every one of us depends for life on some other source.

Actually, that is the very essence of the word *nefesh*. The word describes life that does not initiate, but is dependent. Adam was made a living soul. His life depended on the breath of God that was breathed into him. As 1 Corinthians 15:45 states, "'The first man Adam became a living being [soul].' The last Adam became a life-giving spirit." God granted Jesus to have life in Himself. Jesus gives life.

At the very beginning of this chapter we noted Jesus' words in John 10:10: "I have come that they may have life, and that they may have it more abundantly." All of us are dependent on God for life; and the only channel of eternal life that God has given us is the blood of Jesus. If we want life, we must recognize that it comes to us through the blood of Jesus. The more you learn to meditate on and to honor and to appropriate the blood of Jesus in your life, the fuller and more abundant your life will be.

How do we feed on the blood of Jesus?

I began my ministry in 1946 in the land of Israel in what was then a small Arab village called Ramallah. Although I was never fluent in Arabic, it was the language we used in our home. In this way I learned that when Arabs want to take the Lord's Supper, they say, "Let's drink the blood of Jesus." So I grew up, in a certain sense, with the concept that taking the Lord's Supper is drinking the blood of Jesus. As I understand it, this is one way we appropriate the soul life of the Lord Jesus that He has made available to us.

When Jesus died on the cross and poured out His blood, you see, the life of God was released into the universe. It is available now to anyone who will receive it through faith in Jesus. Up to that time, the life of God had been confined within God.

The thought of what took place when Jesus died on the cross staggers the human mind! In the blood of Jesus freely poured out was released the total life of God, available to us only through His blood. There is no channel of life other than the blood.

During the twenty years I was married to Ruth, we led a very nomadic life. We traveled frequently and seldom spent long residence in any single location. We discovered that we could introduce a measure of stability into our lives by establishing certain practices that we followed every day. One that became very precious to us was receiving Communion together every morning before we became involved in all the activities of the day. As the priest of my home, therefore, I served Communion every morning to Ruth, and we made this confession together: "We thank You that in the blood of Jesus we receive the life of God—divine, eternal, endless life." That is what we believed all those years, and I still believe it today.

Confessing the Exchange

Will you claim this fourth exchange in the form of the following verbal confession?

Jesus died my death that I might share His life.

Thank You, Jesus, for giving me Your life!

Questions for the Study

1. According to John 10:10, why did Jesus come to earth?
2. According to Romans 6:23, what are the wages of sin?
3. According to Leviticus 17:11, what makes atonement for our souls?
4. For us to have life, what must we do?
5. When Jesus died on the cross and poured out His blood, what was released into the universe?
6. Confess with your mouth the exchange given at the end of the chapter.

7

BLESSING IN PLACE
OF CURSE

Now we look at the fifth aspect of the exchange at the cross: moving from curse to blessing. It is stated explicitly in Galatians 3:13–14:

Christ has redeemed us from the curse of the law, having become a curse for us (for it is written, "Cursed is everyone who hangs on a tree"), that the blessing of Abraham might come upon the Gentiles in Christ Jesus, that we might receive the promise of the Spirit through faith.

Here is the exchange: *Every curse that might have come on us came on Jesus instead, that all the blessings due Him might be made available to us.* Jesus was actually made a curse in our place, that we might receive "the blessing of Abraham."

In what ways was Abraham blessed? Genesis 24:1 reveals the answer: "Abraham was old, well advanced in age; and the Lord had blessed Abraham in all things." The blessing of Abraham, then, covers every area of our lives, and that is the blessing that was made available to us through faith in the exchange that took place when Jesus was made a curse for us on the cross.

To begin to analyze the nature of curses and blessings, we need to go back to the beginning of the chapter in which our key verse appears:

> O foolish Galatians! Who has bewitched you that you should not obey the truth, before whose eyes Jesus Christ was clearly portrayed among you as crucified?
>
> Galatians 3:1

A few verses later Paul reminded the Galatian Christians of Him "who supplies the Spirit to you and works miracles among you" (verse 5). In contemporary language we might say these were charismatic, or Spirit-filled, Christians. And yet Paul said they were bewitched. What an amazing statement! Why did he say that?

Because they had lost their vision of the cross. "Jesus Christ was clearly portrayed among you as crucified," Paul wrote, but something had happened to them that had obscured their vision of the cross. In fact, an evil, satanic force had moved in and shut off their understanding of the cross. By using the word *bewitched*—in the Greek, *baskaino*—Paul was calling that force witchcraft.

The Deception of Witchcraft

I will not go into an analysis of witchcraft here, but it is important to understand that being saved or filled with the Holy Spirit or seeing miracles does not guarantee us an exemption from deception. It is still possible for satanic influences to move in among Christians, with the main aim of obscuring the cross. If we lose our vision of the cross—the only basis for God's total provision for us—we no longer have a foundation for His provision.

Also, the cross is where Jesus defeated Satan and his kingdom. "Having disarmed principalities and powers," Paul wrote in Colossians 2:15, "[Jesus] made a public spectacle of them, triumphing over them in [the cross]." Satan can never undo the defeat he received through the cross. But his cunning strategy is to keep Christians from realizing what was accomplished there.

Paul began almost every epistle by thanking God for what He had done for the recipients of that epistle. Even when the apostle was forced to reprove the church at Corinth for incest, adultery and drunkenness at the Lord's table, he started his first epistle to the Corinthians by thanking God for the grace of God given to them (see 1 Corinthians 1:4). When he wrote to the Galatian Christians, however, Paul showed his tremendous concern for them almost immediately: "I marvel that you are turning away so soon . . . to a different gospel" (Galatians 1:6). What was the problem? Not drunkenness or immorality. The problem was legalism. Paul was much more upset about legalism than about a sin of the flesh.

Two Results

The results of this witchcraft were twofold. First, they had become *carnal*. Paul offered a stern warning in Galatians 5:16–21 about the works of the flesh: immorality, impurity, etc. Witchcraft must have opened the way for such sins of the flesh. Having lost the vision of the cross, the Galatians had become very legalistic. They were seeking to achieve righteousness by keeping a set of rules.

Let me give you two simple definitions of legalism.

First, *legalism is the attempt to achieve righteousness with God by keeping a set of rules, which God has disallowed forever.* I was talking once to a large group of Christians and made the casual statement, "Of course, Christianity is not a set of rules." They looked at me in astonishment. I think that if I had said there was no God, they would have been less shocked. Yet the truth is, Christianity is *not* a set of rules. Keeping rules is not the way to achieve righteousness with God.

Second, *legalism is adding any requirement for righteousness to what God has already stated in His Word.* No one has ever been authorized to add to God's requirements. These are very simple and are stated at the end of Romans 4—that we "believe in Him who raised up Jesus our Lord from the dead, who was delivered up because of our offenses, and was raised because of our justification." Remember that justified means "just-as-if-I'd" never sinned! Don't forget that word *justification*! Nothing more is needed. And no one has ever been authorized to add any further requirement. But the Galatian church had become both carnal and legalistic. It had also come under a curse, which is always the end of people who turn away from the Gospel of grace to a gospel of works. Paul summed it up in Galatians 3:10:

> For as many as are of the works of the law are under the curse; for it is written, *"Cursed is everyone who does not continue in all things which are written in the book of the law, to do them."*

When you set out to achieve righteousness with God by keeping a set of laws and then you break any law at any point, you come under that curse. You are obligated to keep the whole law all the time, or else it is of no avail to you for righteousness.

The Way Out

Fortunately Paul did not stop with the problem. He revealed a way out from under the curse.

If you think about the picture of Jesus dying on the cross, you would not want to be under a curse. There He hung in shame and agony, forsaken by His disciples, rejected by His own people, with absolutely nothing in this world, refused by heaven, under supernatural darkness, uttering a cry of agony. That is the full outworking of the curse.

The problem today is that the majority of Christians have no clear concept of what a curse is, how it operates or even how to recognize it. If we are sick, we usually know we are sick. If we are sinning, we probably know we are sinning. But when we are under a curse, we may not understand either the nature of our problem or how to deal with it.

Yet this is what was accomplished by this fifth divine exchange: We can be redeemed from the curse because, on the cross, Jesus was made a curse, that we might be redeemed from the curse and come into the blessing of Abraham, which covers every area of our lives.

Now I will give a general picture of a curse, then explain how to come out from under it.

The Nature of Curses and Blessings

The nature of curses and blessings is a vast subject. I never realized how vast until I got involved in it! I would also say that the lessons I have learned in this context have made a more powerful impact on people than any other message God has ever given me. It is a life-changing revelation.

Curses and blessings are essentially words. They may be written, they may be spoken or they may simply be thought. But they are words charged with supernatural authority and power, as Proverbs 18:21 indicates: "Death and life are in the power of the tongue."

In Deuteronomy 28 Moses gives a list of both blessings and curses. The first 14 verses of the chapter depict blessings. The remaining 54 verses depict curses. It is a long and horrifying list. No person in his right senses would wish to have any part of them.

Blessings and curses dramatically affect and change people—for good or for evil. Frequently they continue from generation to generation until something is done to terminate them. There are blessings and curses in the Bible that have been in effect for nearly four thousand years, and their outworking still continues today.

Why should this concern us? Because there may be problems in our lives for which we cannot find the source, but which can be traced back to previous history, perhaps many generations back. We may be groping with a problem we do not know how to deal with until we can identify its nature. Again, one of the distinctive features of both blessings and curses is that they continue—not necessarily forever, but often for several generations.

In the Ten Commandments, for instance, God said that if we worship false gods or make idols, He will "[visit] the iniquity of the fathers upon the children to the third and fourth generations of those who hate Me" (Exodus 20:5). That is typical of a curse. Having dealt in Southeast Asia with multitudes of people whose ancestors two or three generations back were idol-worshipers, I have witnessed how true this is. I have also seen the tremendous effectiveness of releasing them from that curse!

Here are short summaries of the blessings and the curses in Deuteronomy 28. I suggest you read the chapter for yourself and decide whether you agree with my summary. First the blessings:

1. *Personal exaltation*. By this I mean being lifted up, honored.
2. *Reproductiveness*. I use this word to describe a person who reproduces, or is fruitful, in every area of life, whether physical or financial or relational or creative.
3. *Health*. You probably do not appreciate how much of a blessing health is until you are sick, and then you may wish you had thanked God more often for the blessing of being healthy.
4. *Prosperity, or success*. Prosperity in the Bible does not mean what it does to modern Americans. It is not luxurious living or an abundance of physical pleasures, but accomplishing God's purpose and succeeding in doing His will. In Joshua 1:8 the Lord promised Joshua that whatever he did would prosper and that he would have good success. Yet the leader of the Israelites spent many of the following years in warfare, always exposed to danger, sleeping in open fields and leading the tough life of a soldier in war.
5. *Victory*. Blessing brings victory in every conflict that we enter in the will of God.
6. *Being the head and not the tail*. Some years ago I asked the Lord to tell me the difference between the head and

the tail. He gave me a simple answer: *The head makes the decisions and the tail gets dragged around.* Let me ask you: How you are living—like a head or a tail? Do you make the decisions? Are your plans carried out successfully? Or are you the victim of pressures and forces and circumstances that drag you around, and you do not know what to expect next?

7. *Being above and not beneath.* This goes closely with being the head and not the tail.

The curses from Deuteronomy 28 are the opposite of the blessings:

1. *Humiliation.*
2. *Failure to reproduce, or barrenness* (the opposite of reproductiveness). Almost invariably barrenness is the result of a curse.
3. *Sickness of every kind.* One category of sickness that is particularly indicative of a curse is one that is called hereditary, continuing on from generation to generation.
4. *Poverty and failure.*
5. *Defeat*—just the opposite of the blessing of victory.
6. *Being the tail and not the head.*
7. *Being beneath and not above.*

Seven Indications of a Curse

Now I will give you seven indications of a curse, which I have learned by observation in dealing with people, independently of Deuteronomy 28. (But it is remarkable how much they agree!) If you have only one of these problems, it may or may not be a curse. If you have several of them, you may be almost sure you are under a curse.

1. *Mental or emotional breakdown.*
2. *Repeated or chronic sickness, especially if it is hereditary, which is the nature of a curse.*
3. *Female problems (barrenness, miscarriages, menstrual cramps and a whole host of others).* When I minister to the sick, and a woman comes forward with one of these problems, I simply assume it is a curse, and seldom am I wrong. I have a pile of testimonies of women who have been completely set free from these conditions after a curse over their lives was canceled.
4. *Breakdown of marriage, family alienation.* Some families just cannot stick together. Husbands and wives divorce, remarry and often divorce again. Children, too, are alienated from their parents.
5. *Financial insufficiency.* Most of us go through times of financial hardship. I am no exception. But if you are always struggling, if you never have enough, that is probably a curse.
6. *Being accident-prone.* If you are one of those people to whom accidents always happen—you step off the curb and break your ankle; you are in a car and somebody slams into you—you are probably under a curse. A characteristic phrase would be "Why does it always happen to me?"
7. *A history of suicide or unnatural deaths in a family.*

I have an idea what it is like experientially to be under a curse, since God has plunged me into this ministry and taken me around the world to many places and many people who have served as object lessons.

A curse is like a dark shadow from the past. You probably do not know where it comes from; perhaps it did not even originate in your lifetime. It may have something to do with your family background. It stretches out over your life and shuts out the sunshine of God's blessing. You can see other people around you in the sunlight, but rarely do you ever enjoy the sunshine yourself. You may have no idea what it is from the past that is the cause.

Or you could compare a curse to a long, evil arm stretched out from behind you. Every now and then this thing maliciously trips you up or pushes you out of the way. You have struggled hard to get to a certain point in life where you can say, "Now I've got things together!" Just at that moment, however, something happens and success slips out of your grasp. You go through the painful struggle again and arrive back at the same level, and once again the evil thing trips you up. This becomes a pattern in your life. Perhaps when you look back at your parents or grandparents or some other relative, you recognize this pattern in their lives, too.

A curse does not always make a person obviously unsuccessful. I remember a woman I met in Southeast Asia who was from a royal line, highly educated and successful in her career as a judge. She came up to me after I taught on the subject of blessings and curses.

"I don't fit your description," she said, "because I am not unsuccessful. In fact, I have been successful." But then she added, "I'm frustrated. I believe in Jesus, but I never seem to get the things people are supposed to have who believe in Jesus."

After I spoke with her for a few minutes, I discovered that she was descended from a long line of idol-worshipers, and pointed out to her that this was probably the nature of her problem. This proved to be the case. But when she identified her problem and met God's conditions, we were able to revoke the curse associated with her ancestors' idolatry.

The essence of a curse is summed up in one word: *frustration*. You can be unsuccessful and frustrated, or you can be successful and frustrated. There are many successful yet frustrated people in the world today.

What Causes a Curse?

I will give eight possible causes for a curse coming over a person.

1. Idolatry

The primary cause of all curses is idolatry—breaking the first two of the Ten Commandments. Idolatry, including the whole realm of the occult, inevitably and invariably results in some kind of curse. Those who explore the occult are turning to false gods for the help they should be seeking only from the true God, and they come under the same curse pronounced on a person who makes an idol or worships a false god.

2. False Religion and Secret Societies

The second cause for a curse, similar to the first, is false religion and secret societies. Any religion that rejects the revelation of Scripture and the unique Person and function of Jesus Christ is, by biblical standards, a false religion. I do not need to tell you that the world is full of false religions. I include secret societies because a person who joins a secret society has made a covenant with people who are worshiping false gods. Again and again I have encountered curses related to Freemasonry, and conclude from example after example that any family that has been involved with Freemasonry is liable to be under a curse.

3. *Wrong Attitude toward Parents*

Ephesians 6:2–3 says, "Honor your father and mother, ... that it may be well with you and you may live long on the earth." Honoring your parents does not mean you have to agree with them. They may be very wrong, but you must treat them with respect. A higher proportion of people today probably have a wrong attitude toward their parents than any previous generation in human history.

When young people come to me for help, I always check on their relationship to their parents. You can get saved and manifest the gifts of the Holy Spirit and go to heaven when you die, but without a correct attitude toward your parents, it will never go well with you in this life.

4. *Injustice toward the Weak*

The fourth reason for curses is being unjust toward the weak and helpless. God is on the side of the weak and oppressed. The conspicuous example today is abortion—deliberately taking the life of an unborn child. If ever there was an example of someone weak and helpless, it is an unborn infant. In my opinion, if you intentionally procure an abortion, you have invoked a curse over your life.

5. *Anti-Semitism*

The fifth cause for a curse is hating and speaking against the Jewish people. When God called Abraham, He said, "I will curse him who curses you" (Genesis 12:3). This promise was transferred through Isaac to Jacob and to their descendants. It will never go well for someone who has a wrong attitude toward, or who utters wrong words about, the Jewish people.

One of the most amazing examples of this I know is a close friend of mine, a Palestinian Arab born in Haifa who is now a United States citizen. He recognized that he and all his ancestors, as far back as he could remember, had persistently cursed the Jewish people. When he repented of this, renounced it and was released from the curse, God prospered him—spiritually, in his family and in his business—in an astonishing way. Today he tells people boldly, and his fellow Arabs in particular, that if you want the blessing of God, you must change your attitude toward the Jewish people.

6. *Our Own Words*

Some of the most common curses are self-imposed ones that people pronounce on themselves: "I'll never make good." "This always happens to me." "I just can't handle this kind of situation." When you make a statement like one of these, you are pronouncing a curse on yourself.

I have ministered to scores of people who needed deliverance from the spirit of death because they invoked it by saying some such words as, "I wish I were dead. What's the good of living?" That is an invitation to a spirit of death: "Come in, I am welcoming you." You do not have to give it many invitations! I include a word about release from a spirit of death near the end of this chapter. I am not talking about something small or insignificant, but about something very, very real.

7. *Words from Authority Figures*

Some curses come from people with relational authority, like parents and husbands. Many parents get provoked with their children and say bitter, angry words to them, not considering the implications: "You're so stupid!" or "I can't believe how clumsy you are!" or "You'll never make good." I have prayed with people in their forties and fifties still struggling from the effects of words spoken by a parent when they were youngsters.

Comments made by a husband to his wife can bring a curse, too. It may seem unfair, but it is true. God has given husbands authority over wives. Remember what Jacob said in response to an accusation by his father-in-law that a member of his family had stolen Laban's household idols: "With whomever you find your gods, do not let him live" (Genesis 31:32). He did not know that Rachel, his favorite wife, had stolen them. The next time she gave birth, she actually died under her husband's curse. Of course, she had already transgressed by stealing her father's household gods.

Imagine a husband who says to his wife, "You can't cook! I'm sick of your food. You'll never be able to cook!" Although she is talented and able in many other areas, she falls apart in the kitchen. By the same token, although the husband does not realize it, he is actually pronouncing a curse on himself by saying, "I'm sick of your cooking." For the rest of his life he suffers from indigestion! It sounds humorous, but it really happens.

8. Witch Doctors

The final cause of curses to be considered is witch doctors, or shamans, or *tohungas* (depending on what part of the world you come from). These are practitioners of satanic power. Their power is real, and they can kill. Indeed, many people are killed by witchcraft. Covens of witches in almost every major city in the U.S., and in many smaller cities, pray specifically against Christians and against the marriages of Christian ministers. Their supreme aim: to destroy the Church of Jesus Christ.

Having lived in countries like Palestine and Kenya, where people specialize in satanic power, I know that the witch doctor is recognized as the man with power, to whom people go with their needs and problems. In many countries even people who profess Christianity, if they do not get what they want from God, go to the witch doctor.

How to Be Released

Now we come to the steps to be released from a curse. Thank God for the exchange at the cross!

Each of the following four key words begins with *re*:

1. Recognize

Ask God to show you what your problem is. The whole aim of what I have been saying is to help you to recognize a problem. Perhaps a light has been turned on for you, and now you recognize how you brought a curse on yourself. Or perhaps you see a problem that began with your ancestors.

2. Repent

If you are involved personally in anything evil, repent of it. For instance, you may have been involved in the occult or visited a fortuneteller or played with a Ouija board or studied books on the occult. If so, you need to repent! Or perhaps it was the involvement of your parents, grandparents or other ancestors that opened the door to a curse on your family line. You are not guilty, but you may be suffering the consequences. In order to clear that sin from your background, repent on behalf of whoever was responsible.

3. Renounce

Make the following declaration about the curse, whatever it is: "This is not for me! I have been saved by the blood of Jesus. My faith is in His atonement. On the cross He took every curse that was due to me, that I might receive all the good that is due to Him." In this way you renounce or revoke the curse.

4. Resist

The Bible says, "Submit to God. Resist the devil and he will flee from you" (James 4:7). He will flee only if you have submitted to God first. If you have not, he will laugh in your face. Some Christians have reversed the order: They submit to the devil and resist God! You may be doing that yourself—lying down under Satan's pressures and attacks and letting him walk over you. That does not please God, nor is it humility; it is unbelief.

Take your stand and resist! Say, "I am a child of God. This curse does not belong to me. I have been redeemed by the blood of Jesus out of the hand of the devil."

Psalm 107:2 says, "Let the redeemed of the LORD say so." Your redemption does not really work until you make it your personal testimony. Remember, "They overcame [Satan] by the blood of the Lamb and by the word of their testimony" (Revelation 12:11). Repeat your confession aloud several times:

> I have been redeemed by the blood of Jesus out of the hand of the devil.

If you sense a curse of death over you, begin to proclaim Psalm 118:17. I cannot count the times I have declared this verse, since I often find myself in a spiritual war:

> I shall not die, but live, and declare the works of the LORD.

This declaration can make all the difference for your life.

Confessing the Exchange

Now I want to help you apply this particular exchange of the cross to your life. Perhaps you sense some kind of curse over your life, but you believe Jesus was made a curse on the cross that you might be redeemed from the curse. If you are willing to meet God's conditions, I offer below a written prayer that covers every condition necessary for release from a curse. Say these words:

> Lord Jesus Christ, I believe that You are the Son of God and the only way to God the Father. I believe that You died on the cross for my sins and rose again from the dead. I believe that on the cross You were made sin with my

sinfulness that I might be made righteous with Your righteousness. You were made a curse with any curse that might come upon me, that I might receive the blessing.

And now, Lord, I come to You for deliverance from any such curse. I repent of any sins that have caused it to come, whether committed by me or by my ancestors. I receive Your forgiveness.

I take my stand now against the devil and all his pressures and everything he wants to do against me. In the name of Jesus, I resist him. I refuse to submit any longer to him. In the name of Jesus, I now release myself from any curse over my life. Because of what Jesus did for me on the cross, in His name I release myself, and I receive the release now by faith with thankfulness and praise.

Lord, I thank You now. I praise You now. I believe You are faithful. I believe You are doing what I have asked You to do. I commit my life to You, that from now on Your blessing may rest upon me. Thank You, Lord Jesus! Thank You!

Now take a little while to thank Him in your own words. Receive with thanksgiving what He has done and what He is continuing to do.

Following the steps to be released from a curse and confessing this divine exchange does not automatically solve all your problems from this time on. It does, however, open up a new way of life before you. I have dealt with many people who have been released from curses, some of whom had to fight tremendous battles. The change does not necessarily happen overnight. You must be prepared to continue to resist the devil and to tell him, "I have met the conditions. You have no more claims. Get out of my way—a child of God is coming down the road. Step aside!"

When Satan knows you really mean it, he *will* step aside. So don't be disappointed as you tackle some remaining problems. Know that you have set your face toward the light and that you are progressing in the right direction. I want to assure you, there is hope!

Questions for the Study

1. What is the main aim of witchcraft?
2. What were the two results of witchcraft in the Galatian church?
3. What does Galatians 3:10 tell us about walking under the law and not under grace?
4. Through what means were we redeemed from the curse?
5. What are curses and blessings?
6. Review the seven summaries for the curses listed in Deuteronomy 28. Do you see any of these at work in your own life?
7. Are any of the seven indications of a curse evident in your life?
8. The essence of a curse is summed up in what one word?
9. What are eight possible causes for a curse?
10. What are the four steps to be released from a curse?
11. Pray the prayer at the end of this chapter to be released from any curses that might be frustrating your life.

8

ABUNDANCE IN PLACE
OF POVERTY

We are exploring the sacrifice of Jesus on the cross—one perfect, complete, all-sufficient sacrifice that covers the needs of every human being for time and for eternity. I have been unfolding to you the truth that the essence of the sacrifice was an exchange in which all the evil due to us came on Jesus, that all the good due to Jesus might be offered to us. We cannot earn this. As Ephesians 2:8 says, "By grace you have been saved through faith." Grace covers everything Jesus did for us on the cross.

Having dealt with five aspects of the exchange, we should recapitulate them in order to keep them fresh in our minds:

1. Jesus was punished that we might be forgiven.
2. Jesus was wounded that we might be healed.
3. Jesus was made sin with our sinfulness that we might be made righteous with His righteousness.

4. Jesus died our death that we might share His life.
5. Jesus was made a curse that we might receive the blessing.

Now we will explore another facet of this divine exchange:

You know the grace of our Lord Jesus Christ, that though He was rich, yet for your sakes He became poor, that you through His poverty might become rich.

2 Corinthians 8:9

We can articulate the exchange like this: *Jesus endured our poverty that we might share His abundance.*

Would you agree that poverty is a bad thing? There are some Christians who practice *voluntary* poverty, and I respect their convictions. But in most cases poverty is enforced not by choice but by necessity. I have traveled much of the earth and seen poverty in many different nations, and to me poverty is a curse.

The alternative to poverty is riches—but I prefer to say "abundance." I do not believe it is a mark of spirituality for a Christian to drive a Cadillac or Mercedes or to live in a house with a swimming pool. I do believe, however, that God offers us abundance, which means having enough for our own needs and something left over to give others. That is the level of God's provision.

In 2 Corinthians 9:8 Paul sums up the level of God's provision for His servants:

God is able to make all grace abound toward you, that you, always having all sufficiency in all things, may have an abundance for every good work.

That is an amazing verse! In the original Greek text the word *all* occurs five times and the word *abound* or *abun-*

dance twice. That is the level of God's provision for His servants.

But notice that it is received only through grace. It is not something we can deserve or earn. It is received purely by faith on the basis of Christ's sacrifice for us on the cross.

But if you are like me, you may have to wage a mental battle to receive this truth. As a youth I was not very religious, but for ten years, while at school in Britain, I was compelled to attend church eight times a week. At that time I formed the impression that Christians had better expect to be both poor and miserable. If you have something of the same background, you may need to ask God to release your mind from captivity to traditional thinking.

In that great chapter on blessings and curses, Deuteronomy 28, we find these words:

> "All these curses shall come upon you . . . because you did not obey the voice of the LORD your God. . . . Because you did not serve the LORD your God with joy and gladness of heart, for the abundance of everything, therefore you shall serve your enemies, whom the LORD will send against you, in hunger, in thirst, in nakedness, and in need of everything. . . ."
>
> verses 45, 47–48

When we fail, through unbelief or disobedience, to serve God joyfully in our abundance, God says we will experience four things: *hunger, thirst, nakedness* and *the need of all things.* Put them together and what do you have? Absolute poverty.

Let me share with you a revelation that came to me many years ago when I was in New Zealand. The people who had invited my first wife and me had assured us they would cover all our expenses. But when we arrived, they did not have the money to cover our fare. "You'll have to preach for an offering," they told me.

As I was preaching about these verses involving the curse and the blessing, the Holy Spirit gave me a mental picture of Jesus on the cross. The curse of poverty, He showed me, was fulfilled in Jesus. He was hungry; He had not eaten for 24 hours. He was thirsty; one of the last things He said was, "I thirst." He was naked, as they had taken all His clothes from Him. And when He died He owned precisely nothing. He was buried in a borrowed robe and in a borrowed tomb.

As I was speaking that day, the truth came to me that, on the cross, Jesus exhausted the poverty curse. It was not that He was poor. Before Jesus went to the cross, He did not carry a lot of cash but He always had what He needed. Any man who can feed five thousand men (plus women and children) on a hilltop is not poor! To borrow an expression from our contemporary culture, Jesus carried His Father's credit card and it was honored everywhere! To suggest that Jesus was poor before He went to the cross is misleading.

On the cross, however, Jesus not only endured, but He exhausted the poverty curse. There is nothing left of that curse after you have been hungry, thirsty, naked and in need of all things. You cannot be more poor than that!

This revelation somehow broke through to those people in New Zealand. There were only three or four hundred of them, and they were not particularly wealthy. Yet they gave so abundantly that it covered every expense for Lydia and me for the rest of our time there, and for our journey there and back. They had received a revelation that on the cross, Jesus exhausted the poverty curse that we might be blessed with abundance.

Three Levels of Provision

There are three levels of provision: *insufficiency, sufficiency* and *abundance.* Insufficiency means you do not have enough for what you need. If you need $100 of groceries and have only $75, you are shopping out of insufficiency. If you have $100, you are shopping out of sufficiency. If you have $125, you are shopping out of abundance.

Abundance comes from a Latin word meaning "a wave that flows over." You should be a person who has a wave from God that flows over you.

Why does God want all His children to have abundance? Listen to Paul addressing the elders of the church at Ephesus:

> "I have shown you in every way, by laboring like this, that you must support the weak. And remember the words of the Lord Jesus, that He said, 'It is more blessed to give than to receive.'"
>
> Acts 20:35

God has no favorites. He provides abundance that we may not only receive, but give, and thus receive the greater blessing. I do not believe God wants any of His children to be without that greater blessing of giving.

Giving is an important part of the Christian life. This does not mean that we all give large amounts. But God commanded His people, Israel, in the Old Testament, "None shall appear before Me empty-handed" (Exodus 34:20). And Psalm 96:8 says, "Bring an offering, and come into His courts." Do not come to God empty-handed.

But remember, God does not need your tips! When the offering basket comes around, do not reach into your pocket, find the smallest amount you can and put that in. That is not honoring God. You do not have to give, but if you do, give in a way that honors Him. Remember, giving is part of worship. If we cannot worship as we give, we ought not to give at all.

In my five years in east Africa, I saw that when God touches people's hearts, they love to give. Scripture says God loves a "hilarious" giver (a literal translation of 2 Corinthians 9:7). I certainly saw some hilarious givers in Africa. Since most of them had little money, they would march up to the front of the church with an offering of, say, coffee beans on their heads. Later God would touch them again, and they would return to the front, this time, perhaps, with some corncobs. Then God would *really* touch them and they would come up with a live chicken. In their giving they were hilarious.

A Higher Order of Riches

Let me add a word of caution or balance. If all your wealth consists only of your house, your portfolio, your Cadillac or your cottage by the lake, remember one thing: When you die, you will take nothing with you. You will step out into eternity a naked soul.

There is a higher order of riches. In Proverbs 8:17–18 wisdom is speaking—that is, the Wisdom of God:

"I love those who love me, and those who seek me diligently will find me. Riches and honor are with me, enduring riches and righteousness."

Note that word *enduring*. Nothing we have in this world is enduring. We cannot take it with us. So what are *enduring riches*?

First of all, whatever we give to the Kingdom of God. Jesus said:

"Everyone who has left houses or brothers or sisters or father or mother or wife or children or lands, for My name's sake, shall receive a hundredfold, and inherit eternal life."

                                                    Matthew 19:29

What we give out of our substance to the Lord, then, becomes enduring riches. A hundredfold return on your giving equals ten thousand percent—a good rate of interest!

However, it is not always material abundance with which God blesses us. Paul identified two ways we can serve God on this earth, which also constitute enduring riches:

No other foundation can anyone lay than that which is laid, which is Jesus Christ. Now if anyone builds on this foundation with gold, silver, precious stones, wood, hay, straw, each one's work will become clear; for the Day will declare it, because it will be revealed by fire; and the fire will test each one's work, of what sort it is. If anyone's work which he has built on it endures, he will receive a reward. If anyone's work is burned, he will suffer loss; but he himself will be saved, yet so as through fire.

                                            1 Corinthians 3:11–15

Paul gives examples of two kinds of service we can offer to the Lord. One is large in quantity but low in value: wood, hay, straw. The other kind of service—gold, silver and precious stones—is much smaller in quantity but withstands the fire and stands the test of time. Take care that you are not laying up vast quantities of wood, hay and straw, because a fire is coming that will consume these in an instant.

Enduring riches are the lives we bless with the truth of God's Word and with the power of the Holy Spirit, which produces Christian character. In this way we build men and women of God, but usually not in large quantities. Despite our terrible tendency in the Church to focus on numbers, the issue is not how many members a church has, but how many disciples it nurtures. Jesus never told us to get church members; He instructed us to make disciples. I have observed in the course of a long life in God's service that if you make disciples, you will usually start with a small number, as Jesus Himself did. But they will be self-reproducing. In the long run you will end up with a lot, and it will be quality, not quantity.

A Right Perspective

I close this chapter with two Scriptures that put God's provision for abundance into perspective.

The first is Proverbs 13:7: "There is one who makes himself rich, yet has nothing; and one who makes himself poor, yet has great riches." Some deliberately turn away from the material wealth of this world, making themselves poor, while in the spiritual realm they have great riches. I think Paul was one of these.

His testimony in 2 Corinthians 6:4 is the second Scripture. It begins: "In all things we commend ourselves as ministers of God," followed by a long list of what he and his co-workers had experienced, most of which are not on the curriculum of a normal Bible college. They commended themselves in patience, tribulations, needs, distresses, stripes, imprisonments, tumults, labors, sleeplessness and fasting (see verses 4–5).

Paul went on to enumerate other ways he and his co-workers had approved themselves as ministers of God:

As unknown, and yet well known; as dying, and behold we live; as chastened, and yet not killed; as sorrowful, yet always rejoicing; *as poor, yet making many rich; as having nothing, and yet possessing all things.*

verses 9–10, emphasis added

Poverty is a curse. God's provision is abundance. But do not focus merely on the material realm, because when you die, that will be the end of it. To those whose priorities are right, God offers greater and more enduring riches.

Claiming This Exchange

Once again let's put this exchange in the form of a verbal confession:

Jesus endured my poverty that I might share His abundance.

Thank You, Jesus, for giving me Your abundance.

Questions for the Study

1. What is the level of God's provision for His servants?
2. If we are walking in unbelief or disobedience, what four things does God say we will experience?
3. How did Jesus deal with the curse of poverty?
4. What are the three levels of provision?
5. Why does God provide abundance?
6. What are enduring riches?
7. Confess with your mouth the exchange given at the end of this chapter.

9

GLORY IN PLACE OF SHAME

Now we come to two aspects of the exchange at the cross that provide emotional healing for the wounds of shame and rejection. We have read the Scripture several times, "By His stripes [wounds] we are healed" (Isaiah 53:5). This is true in the physical realm, but also in the emotional realm.

There are various emotional wounds, of course, and healing for all of them is provided through the cross. But shame and rejection are two of the most common and deepest emotional wounds that humanity suffers.

First, shame. What is the opposite of shame? Glory! On the cross Jesus suffered the wound of shame to the ultimate that we might be healed from it. *Jesus endured our shame that we, in turn, might share His glory.* In this chapter we will discuss the shame of the crucifixion, deal with some of the causes of shame in people today and discuss how we can find healing.

I have had no greater privilege in my ministry than to see people healed from the wounds of shame and rejection. God's remedy is not just theory or theology; it works! I believe that if you accept the principle that healing is provided through the substitutionary sacrifice of Jesus, you will be able to find healing for yourself. And if you have a ministry of teaching or counseling, you will have the privilege of leading others into healing.

I have learned from many years of counseling and ministry that shame is one of the most common emotional problems of God's people. Furthermore believers are ashamed to let others know they have the problem. In a sense shame shuts you up in a prison.

We turn, as a scriptural basis, to Hebrews 2:10:

> It was fitting for Him [God the Father], for whom are all things and by whom are all things, in bringing many sons [that is, you and me] to glory, to make the captain of their salvation [that is, Jesus] perfect through sufferings.

God permitted Jesus to endure those sufferings that we might come into His fullness. Notice God's purpose: *to bring many sons to glory*. If you are a believing child of God, you are bound for glory. On the cross Jesus endured your shame that you might share His glory.

Hebrews 12:2 also brings out the theme of Christ enduring our shame. It admonishes us to keep

> looking unto Jesus, the author and finisher of our faith [or the originator and perfecter of our faith], who for the joy that was set before Him endured the cross, *despising the shame*, and has sat down at the right hand of the throne of God.

> emphasis added

On the cross Jesus endured shame—such shame as we can hardly imagine. But He did not let it deter Him. With His mind focused on the joy that was set before Him, there was absolutely nothing that could turn Him away from His purpose. This was the joy that was set before Him: bringing many sons to glory. In order to bring you and me and millions of others like us to glory, He endured the shame of the cross.

The Shame of the Crucifixion

Many years ago my first wife and I became involved in helping two Jewish women who had escaped from the Soviet Union. I went to much pain and trouble to help them. One day I was complaining to myself as I was toiling up a steep hill in Haifa on a hot day, thinking how much I had to go through for those two ladies. (They were very grateful for the help, by the way.) God impressed 2 Timothy 2:10 on my heart:

> I endure all things for the sake of the elect [God's chosen ones], that they also may obtain the salvation which is in Christ Jesus with eternal glory.

I realized that I was enduring just a very little inconvenience—not to be compared to what Jesus endured on the cross—and I was greatly humbled.

There was no form of death more shameful than crucifixion. It was the lowest form of punishment for the most debased criminals. They took all of Jesus' clothing away from Him, and He hung naked before the eyes of the people. Passersby mocked Him. What He endured is summed up in one word: *shame.* Christ endured the shame because He knew that, through it, He could bring us to glory.

The New Testament gives us little subjective information about what Jesus endured on the cross. In fact, you could not say it more shortly. All four gospel accounts say simply, "They crucified Him." The Old Testament psalmists and prophets, however, offer a wonderful unfolding revelation of what went on inside Jesus.

Returning to Isaiah 53, the great atonement chapter, we look at the emphasis on the shame that Jesus experienced:

> He is despised and rejected by men, a Man of sorrows [literally, *pains*] and acquainted with grief [*sickness*]. And we hid, as it were, our faces from Him; He was despised, and we did not esteem Him.
>
> verse 3

I understand this to mean that we averted our eyes from Him because the sight was so horrible. The previous verse says that Jesus had "no form or comeliness"—He lost even the form of a human being. All His wounds, bruises and putrefying sores were exposed to the view of those who hated Him, to those who were responsible for His crucifixion, as well as to idle passersby.

Psalm 69 is one of those wonderful messianic psalms that refer not simply to David, who spoke or wrote the words, but also to the Messiah Himself. From verse 7:

> For Your sake I have borne reproach; shame has covered my face.

Here we understand a little more of what Jesus endured on the cross. Have you ever noticed that people who suffer from shame find it hard to look you in the face? Shame covered the face of the suffering Servant.

In the first two verses of Psalm 69 we catch a further glimpse:

> Save me, O God! For the waters have come up to my neck [Hebrew, *to my soul*]. I sink in deep mire, where there is no standing.

Alone and unsupported, Jesus was sinking deeper and deeper in the slimy filthiness of the world's sin.

Four additional verses from Psalm 69 are applied in the New Testament specifically to Jesus. First, Jesus quoted verse 4 about Himself (see John 15:25):

> Those who hate me without a cause are more than the hairs of my head.

And verse 8:

> I have become a stranger to my brothers, and an alien to my mother's children.

Remember that Jesus' own people, and even His own family, rejected Him (see Mark 3:21; John 7:3–5).

Verse 9 is applied to Jesus' cleansing the Temple in John 2:17:

> Zeal for Your house has eaten me up, and the reproaches of those who reproach You have fallen on me.

Finally verse 21 was fulfilled when Jesus hung on the cross (see Matthew 27:34, 48):

> They also gave me gall for my food, and for my thirst they gave me vinegar to drink.

This never happened to David, but the Spirit of Messiah in him was speaking in the first person of things that Jesus would experience on the cross.

In 1 Peter 1:10–11 the apostle explains how the prophets of the Old Testament could speak in the first person of things that never happened to them, but that were fulfilled in the life of Jesus:

> Of this salvation the prophets have inquired and searched carefully, who prophesied of the grace that would come to you, searching what, or what manner of time, the Spirit of Christ who was in them was indicating when He testified beforehand the sufferings of Christ and the glories that would follow.

Now let's look at the actual description of the crucifixion in Matthew 27:35, which quotes Psalm 22, another messianic psalm:

> They crucified Him, and divided His garments, casting lots, that it might be fulfilled which was spoken by the prophet: *"They divided My garments among them, and for My clothing they cast lots."*

I marvel at the restraint of the gospel writers, who simply said, "They crucified Him." They did not give us a picture of blood or of agony. Any modern writer asked to depict the crucifixion would have spent pages on the details. But the New Testament leaves it to the Holy Spirit to add what we need to know.

Now picture those soldiers dividing the garments of Jesus among themselves. It is generally agreed that a man in those days had four items of clothing. Since there were also four soldiers, each soldier took one item; but they cast lots for the seamless robe, which was too fine to divide among them. See how exact the Scripture is! The end result: Jesus was exposed—totally naked on the cross.

What about the women who followed Jesus? The only three who came close to the cross were His mother, Mary; His aunt, Mary, the wife of Clopas; and Mary Magdalene (see John 19:25). The rest remained at a distance. Again, I believe this indicates that Jesus was exposed naked to the world. Our pretty pictures of the crucifixion—portraying Him with a loincloth, a little blood on His hands and feet and a nicely adjusted crown of thorns on His head—give us no concept of what actually took place.

Yet Jesus endured our shame that we might be delivered from shame, and share His glory.

Why Do People Experience Shame?

There are a number of different reasons why people experience shame.

One is humiliating experiences in the past. These often happen to us in school where, for some reason, a pupil is made a spectacle to the whole class. In the old days a teacher gave a student a dunce's cap and made him or her stand in the corner. Classroom discipline is important, but that particular punishment exposed students to shame. A sensitive child might have been wounded inwardly for the rest of his life.

Another reason for shame is memories we carry of what we did before we knew the Lord—things that were shameful and degrading. Sometimes I wonder how I could ever have done some of the things I did.

Perhaps the most common single cause of shame today is sexual molestation of children. Statistics in America today are frightening. Research indicates that one of every four girls and one of every five boys has been molested before the age of twelve. If you think that this does not happen inside the church, you are wrong. When I first began to discover what things were like "under the lid" of the church, I could hardly bear what I discovered. I do not want to be negative, but sexual abuse happens to deacons' children and to preachers' children. No area of the church is exempt.

If you are involved in counseling, you may be ministering to people who bear the wound of shame—some of whom carry it because of molestation in childhood. But remember, these emotional wounds were taken care of at the cross. That is why Jesus was exposed there naked.

Or perhaps you yourself carry this wound of shame. If so, let the Holy Spirit deal with you. He is so gracious, so tender, so tactful and yet so truthful. Don't run away from this issue. Remember the good news: On the cross Jesus endured all the shame that could ever happen to any one of us. He bore it on Himself. He removed it. He took it out of the way.

Two passages in the book of Job speak of lifting up your face to God. First, Job 11:14–15:

"If iniquity were in your hand, and you put it far away . . .
then surely you could lift up your face without spot; yes,
you could be steadfast, and not fear."

Another thing I have observed about people struggling with shame is that they seldom lift their faces up to God in prayer. They pray with their faces turned downward. Why is this? Shame. One of the marks of shame is an unwillingness to look God or man in the face.

But Job 22:26 describes what happens to a person who has been delivered from shame:

Then you will have your delight in the Almighty, and lift up your face to God.

This can be your experience!

Confessing This Exchange

How do you get healed from the wound of shame? By faith. It is very simple. Thank Jesus that He bore your shame so that you might be released from it. Giving thanks is the simplest expression of faith.

Right now, for a moment, shut yourself in with God. Pray these words:

> God, if there is shame in my heart and life that keeps me from lifting up my face to You, I want to be set free, that I can be unashamed. I believe that Jesus bore my shame that I might share His glory.

Let the presence of God rest on you and release you from the bondage of shame. Then lift up your face to God and thank Him for allowing you to share Christ's glory.

In 1 Peter 1:10–11 the apostle describes the outworking of this exchange. Speaking of the prophets of the Old Testament, he says:

> Of this salvation the prophets have inquired and searched carefully, who prophesied of the grace that would come to you, searching what, or what manner of time, the Spirit of Christ who was in them was indicating when He testified beforehand the sufferings of Christ and *the glories* that would follow.

> emphasis added

Lay hold of this fact: Jesus endured your shame that you may share His glory. It is God's provision for you—both in this life and in the next!

Questions for the Study

1. According to Hebrews 2:10, why did Jesus have to endure suffering?
2. What does shame do to a person?
3. Why did Jesus endure the shame of the cross?
4. What are some of the reasons people experience shame?
5. What is one of the marks of shame?
6. If you have shame and want to start on the road to healing, pray the prayer found on page 114.

10

ACCEPTANCE IN PLACE OF REJECTION

LOVE
G

In the previous chapter we dealt with the emotional wound of shame. We saw that *Jesus endured our shame that we in turn might share His glory*. In this chapter we deal with rejection.

What is the opposite of rejection? Acceptance. Here is the exchange: *Jesus endured our rejection that we might have His acceptance.*

I admit that rejection is not an issue I have struggled with personally. In fact, my perspective has been the opposite. I have always had the attitude (which I am not saying is a good one!) that "if you don't like me, that's your problem." I have learned about rejection objectively—and, I must say, with surprise. At first I could not believe what people went through! As I ministered to people suffering from rejection, God taught me about it, and I came to a special place of compassion and understanding.

(Rejection can be described as the sense of being unwanted and unloved. I have explained it this way: You are always on the outside looking in. Other people get in; somehow you never do.)

I would not endorse all of Mother Teresa's theology, but I certainly agree with her diagnosis of humanity's basic problem: (*The worst sickness is not being loved.*)

First John 4:19 says, "We love Him because He first loved us." How profoundly true! We cannot love God until His love awakens love in us. This is also true of us in relation to human love. We are incapable of loving unless love has been awakened in us by someone else's love. A person who has never been loved does not know how to love. Multitudes of people who suffer from rejection want to love but are unable to, because love has never been awakened in them.

Causes for Rejection

Rejection, I believe, is the most prevalent emotional wound in our contemporary culture. There are a number of reasons for this. One is *the breakdown of family relationships.*

Every baby is born into the world with one supreme need: to love and be loved. A baby needs to be cuddled and held, knowing instinctively that you take pleasure in holding him or her in your arms. Mere abstract love cannot meet the need of a baby; love has to be expressed actively.

I further believe—and psychologists have recently been coming to this conclusion—that for every child the love of a father is irreplaceable. I am not by any means belittling a mother's love, which is unique. But security, for an infant, is found in the father's arms. When a tiny baby is held by the father, he or she almost seems to be saying, "Anything can happen all around me, but I'm safe in these strong arms that hold me and love me." In our contemporary society, however, because family relationships have broken down, many babies do not experience this kind of loving acceptance from a father.

Sometimes the problem goes back to *rejection before birth.* Over the years I have talked with people who needed to be delivered from a spirit of rejection that came on them in their mother's womb.

Here is a mother struggling to feed her four children. Now she discovers she is pregnant again. Perhaps she resents this unwelcome event. She lacks the time, money or other resources to raise this child. She may think (or even say), "I wish I weren't pregnant. How I wish this baby weren't coming!" She does not have to say anything aloud, because the little person inside—and bear in mind, it *is* a person—knows that he or she is not welcome. That baby is then born with a spirit of rejection.

Many years back, in the ministry of deliverance, I began to notice that Americans of a certain age frequently tended to need deliverance from rejection. I set out to learn when they were born. The answer was 1929, 1930 and following. Being British, I did not know what had happened in 1929. But when most Americans hear the year 1929, they say, "Oh, the Great Depression!" My mind pieced together what must have happened in the hearts of many still unborn children during those years.

Another main cause of rejection is *the breakup of marriages.* Most of us know that fifty percent of marriages today end in divorce, and the wounds are usually felt by both parties. Some women imagine that they are the only ones who suffer, but that is not true. A man can feel rejection just as deeply.

Isaiah 54:6 is addressed to Zion, but it applies as a pattern to all rejected wives—and beyond that, to all who have suffered personal rejection:

> "The LORD will call you back as if you were a wife deserted and distressed in spirit—a wife who married young, only to be rejected," says your God.
>
> NIV

Who can number the people in our world today who feel rejected because a marriage broke up? Imagine a woman who has given everything to her husband, determined to make a successful marriage. And then he goes off with another woman! I recognize that there is no way for me to understand what she has gone through, to put myself in her place, to feel what she feels. How wonderful that God can—and does!

Other causes of rejection include even *physical appearance*. Most young women today have to be slim to be popular, which is ridiculous! A girl may be a little plumper or quieter than her schoolmates, or wear the "wrong" clothes, and feel rejected. A boy may be a little shorter or slower or less good at sports. It does not take much to make a person feel rejected.

We can easily identify—and perhaps identify with—the problem. Now let's look at the solution. Once again it is provided by Jesus, who on the cross endured total rejection.

Jesus' Rejection on the Cross

Isaiah 53:3 offers a prophetic picture of the cross painted seven hundred years before it happened:

He is despised and rejected by men, a Man of sorrows [or *pains*] and acquainted with grief [or *sickness*]. And we hid, as it were, our faces from Him; He was despised, and we did not esteem Him.

The suffering Servant was "rejected by men." John says, "He came to His own, and His own did not receive Him" (John 1:11). His own brothers, His mother's children, rejected Him. We also see this in Psalm 69, the messianic psalm that we looked at in the last chapter:

I have become a stranger to my brothers, and an alien to my mother's children.

Psalm 69:8

Notice that it refers to "my mother's children," not "my father's children." Many messianic prophecies speak about the mother of the Messiah but not about the father. The conception and birth of the Messiah, of course, were unique.

All those of us who have experienced this kind of rejection need to realize that Jesus Himself experienced it, too. His own family and His own people rejected Him. Only a lonely little group of three women stood by Him to the end.

But that was not the final act. To be rejected by men was painful, but to be rejected by His heavenly Father was the ultimate rejection. Matthew 27:45–47 offers a description of the closing moments of Jesus on the cross:

From the sixth hour until the ninth hour there was darkness over all the land. And about the ninth hour Jesus cried out with a loud voice, saying, "Eli, Eli, lama sabachthani?" that is, *"My God, My God, why have You forsaken Me?"*

Some of those who stood there, when they heard that, said, "This Man is calling for Elijah!"

Not understanding the language, they thought *Eli* was the name of Elijah.

Immediately one of them ran and took a sponge, filled it with sour wine and put it on a reed, and offered it to Him to drink.

verse 48

Twice, while on the cross, Jesus was offered something to drink. Mark 15:23 records that He was offered wine to drink mingled with myrrh, but He refused it. Myrrh was a painkiller that could to some degree have alleviated His suffering. Apparently He had set His heart to endure the agony without alleviation.

Then, in His final moments, Jesus was given sour wine or vinegar, which was bitter. This may have been intended to keep Him from losing consciousness. By accepting this sour wine, Jesus symbolically drained the bitter cup of rejection to its dregs. No human being has ever experienced such total rejection as Jesus experienced on the cross.

The rest said, "Let Him alone; let us see if Elijah will come to save Him." And Jesus cried out again with a loud voice, and yielded up His spirit.

Matthew 27:49–50

For the first time in the history of the universe, the Son of God prayed and there came no answer from the Father. Why? Because (as we saw in chapter 5) Christ had been made sin with our sinfulness, and God had to deal with Him as He deals with sin. God had to reject Him—to refuse to accept Him—and so He died not of crucifixion, but of a broken heart.

How Jesus Actually Died

Remember, the New Testament tells us nothing of what went on inside Jesus, but the Old Testament does. Let us return to Psalm 69:

> Reproach has broken my heart, and I am full of heaviness; I looked for someone to take pity, but there was none; and for comforters, but I found none. They also gave me gall for my food, and for my thirst they gave me vinegar to drink.
>
> Psalm 69:20–21

Normally crucifixion would not have caused so quick a death. As a matter of fact, this is borne out in the New Testament:

> Joseph of Arimathea, a prominent council member, who was himself waiting for the kingdom of God, coming and taking courage, went in to Pilate and asked for the body of Jesus. *Pilate marveled that He was already dead*; and summoning the centurion, he asked him if He had been dead for some time. So when he found out from the centurion, he granted the body to Joseph.
>
> Mark 15:43–45, emphasis added

Normally speaking, then, Jesus should not have been dead so soon. The two thieves had to be put to death by the soldiers. So we may surmise from Psalm 69 and from the New Testament record that Jesus did not die of crucifixion, although that would have killed Him ultimately, but of a broken heart. It is important to see that. What broke His heart? Rejection by His Father—the ultimate rejection. He endured this in order that we might have acceptance.

We return to Matthew 27:50–51:

> Jesus cried out again with a loud voice, and yielded up His spirit. Then, behold, the veil of the temple was torn in two from top to bottom.

The veil in the Temple, which separated a holy God from sinful man, was torn in two, declaring that we can have acceptance. It was torn from top to bottom so that nobody should ever imagine that man did it. It was done by God. That torn veil is the Father's invitation to every person who believes in Jesus: "Come in; you are welcome. My Son has endured your rejection that I may offer you My acceptance."

> Blessed be the God and Father of our Lord Jesus Christ, who has blessed us with every spiritual blessing in the heavenly places in Christ, just as He chose us in Him before the foundation of the world . . .
>
> Ephesians 1:3–4

Notice that this ultimate choice is not ours but God's. Do not imagine that you are saved because you chose to be! You are saved because God chose and you responded to His choice. You might change your mind, but God does not.

> . . . that we should be holy and without blame before Him in love . . .
>
> verse 4

What a tremendous thought! If it were not based on God's choice, I would never have faith that I could be holy and without blame before Him in love. It is God's choice, however, and not ours.

There is a great deal of wrong emphasis in contemporary presentations of the Gospel, in which everything depends on what we do. It is true that we have to choose, but we would never be able to choose if God had not chosen us in the first place. You will find you are much more secure as a Christian when you are not basing your relationship with God on what you do, but on what God has done. God is more dependable than you and I!

> ... having predestined us to adoption as sons by Jesus Christ to Himself, according to the good pleasure of His will, to the praise of the glory of His grace, by which He made us accepted in the Beloved.
>
> Ephesians 1:5–6

Acceptance in the Beloved—surely this is the ultimate acceptance! Modern translations use different words for *accepted*, but the word used in Ephesians, *charitoo*, means "to make graceful or gracious" or "highly favored." The same word is used when the angel Gabriel said to the virgin Mary, "Rejoice, highly favored one" (Luke 1:28).

Being highly favored is even better than being accepted. Understand this: God has no second-class children. All His children are not only welcome but, through Jesus Christ, highly favored.

Who planned all this? God did!

Accepting Jesus' Work

A little incident many years ago made this truth vivid to me. I was due to preach in a big camp meeting and was in danger of being late. Hurrying across the campground, I ran into a woman—or, rather, she ran into me.

As we straightened ourselves out after the collision, she said, "Oh, Mr. Prince, I was praying that if God wanted me to speak to you, we'd meet."

"Well, we've met!" I said. "But I can only give you two minutes, or I'll be late for my preaching."

In one minute she began to tell me all her woes and problems. At the end of that time I stopped her.

"I can't give you any more time," I said. "Say this prayer with me."

I did not tell her what I was going to pray, nor did I diagnose her condition. I simply led her in a prayer that went something like this:

O God, I thank You that You really love me, that I really am Your child, that You really are my Father, that I belong to the best family in the universe. I am not unwanted; I am not rejected. I am accepted. You love me and I love You. Thank You, God.

After that we parted. I made it to my preaching assignment and forgot about the incident.

A month later I got a letter from this woman. After describing the incident and where we had met, so that she could be sure I knew who she was, she wrote something like this: "Praying that prayer with you has completely changed my life. I am a different person."

What happened? She passed from rejection to acceptance—not by anything she did, or by trying harder or improving herself or praying more. She was released from rejection simply by accepting what Jesus had done for her on the cross.

Claiming This Exchange

The worst thing you can do for people struggling with rejection is to tell them to do more and try harder. They will never believe they have done enough, no matter how much more they do.

Here is the wonderful thing: God loves us. God loves you individually. He loves me, too, incredible though it may seem. In Christ we are His children. We belong to the best family in the universe. We have nothing to be ashamed of. We are not second class, not unwanted. We are accepted.

To appropriate this marvelous exchange, confess it with your mouth:

Jesus endured my rejection that I might have His acceptance.

If you really believe this, say: "Thank You, Father, that You really love me, and that You gave Your only Son for me. You are my Father. Heaven is my home. I am part of the best family in the universe. I am secure in Your unconditional love and care. Thank You, Lord!"

Questions for the Study

1. Rejection can be described as what kind of feeling?
2. What are some of the reasons we experience rejection?
3. To what degree did Jesus experience rejection?
4. According to Ephesians 1:5–6, what has God done through Jesus for us?
5. Pray the prayer above and confess with your mouth the exchange.

11

THE NEW MAN IN PLACE
OF THE OLD MAN

Until now we have been dealing with what the cross
has done for us. Of course, people are glad for this,
but many Christians stop here. All their praying is
asking for more and more and more! Their Christianity becomes shallow and unsatisfying because that is not God's
end purpose.

So now we move into another aspect of the work of the
cross: not what the cross can do *for* us, but what it can do *in*
us. We will examine God's dealings with what is called *the old
man*. This is the doorway to the next section, which covers
what the cross needs to do in us.

First we need to form a clearer idea of what the old man
is. He is not—as you might think—your father! The New
Testament speaks about two men: the old man and the new
man. They are never named, never called George or Henry

or Bill. Yet they are two of the most important characters in the New Testament.

The old man, as I understand it, is the sinful nature we have inherited by our descent from Adam. Some people call it the "old Adam," which is legitimate. Adam never had any children until he was a rebel. Every descendant of Adam, therefore, is born with a rebel within. It does not matter how clever you are, or how young, or how old. There is a rebel inside every descendant of Adam.

You can see this with little children. Because I am the adoptive father of nine girls, I have some experience in dealing with girls. A little girl about the age of two is the sweetest, cutest creature. You could not believe that ice cream would melt in her mouth. But if you say, "Come here," she may turn and run in the opposite direction! Even at that early age the rebel is manifesting himself.

The Bible calls this rebel the old man. God's plan is to replace the old man with the new man. We might say it this way:

On the cross our old man was put to death that the new man might come to life in us instead.

In Matthew 3:10—the verse that really introduces the Gospel—John the Baptist, the forerunner sent before Jesus, declares, "Even now the ax is laid to the root of the trees." The word *radical*, derived from the Latin word *radix*, root, means "that which deals with the root." Of all the messages that have ever come to humanity, the most radical is the Gospel. Many people have a superficial version of the Gospel. But God does not just chop off the branches; He does not even just cut down the trunk. He deals with the root.

Attending to the Root

When God led me into the ministry of deliverance, I dealt mainly with branches at the top of the tree—addictions, obvious fleshly sins that religious people do not like. Soon I realized, however, that every addiction is a branch growing out of a bigger branch. If you lop off only the addiction branches, you have not dealt with the root problem. The basic problem of every addiction is frustration. To deal with the addiction, you must discover the frustration that caused the addiction to grow.

Even frustrations, however, are only branches. To deal with the problems of humanity, you must go below the surface to the root. That is what John the Baptist said: "Even now the ax is laid to the root of the trees." What is the root?

Isaiah tells us plainly:

> All we like sheep have gone astray; we have turned, every one, to his own way; and the LORD has laid on Him [Jesus] the iniquity of us all.
>
> Isaiah 53:6

There is our root problem: our rebellion against God. There is a rebel who resides inside every one of us. He may be a Communist rebel, an alcoholic rebel, even a nice religious rebel, but he is still a rebel. God has only one remedy for the rebel. He does not send him to Sunday school or church, or teach him the Golden Rule, or even tell him to memorize Scripture. He *executes* him. Execution is God's solution.

But the message of mercy is that the execution took place in Jesus on the cross. According to Romans 6:6–7:

> Our old man was crucified with Him, that the body of
> sin might be done away with, that we should no longer
> be slaves of sin. For he who has died has been freed
> from sin.

Paul is not speaking of your past sins. He is dealing with the rebel inside you *now*. You can go to church and say a prayer and get your sins forgiven. But if you walk out of church with the rebel still alive inside you, that rebel will go on sinning. In order to be freed from slavery to sin, we must do more than receive forgiveness for our past sins; we must deal with the rebel inside.

Here is where the death of Jesus on the cross comes in. Our old man was crucified with Him. This is a historical fact. It is true whether or not you know it, or whether or not you believe it. The problem with many Christians is, they do not know it. The crucifixion of your old man with Christ cannot work in your life until you know and believe it. That is what makes this crucifixion real in your experience.

Anyone in whom the old man has not been dealt with is still a slave of sin. Romans 6:6–7, which we just looked at, makes this clear. But the person who has died with Christ "has been freed from sin." The Greek uses the word *justified*. Once you have paid the final penalty, there is no more penalty to pay. The law can demand nothing more from you after you are dead.

> Now if we died with Christ, we believe that we shall also
> live with Him, knowing that Christ, having been raised
> from the dead, dies no more. Death no longer has domin-
> ion over Him. For the death that He died, He died to sin
> once for all; but the life that He lives, He lives to God.
>
> verses 8–10

That is the historical fact. Now here is the application:

Likewise you also, reckon yourselves to be dead indeed to sin, but alive to God in Christ Jesus our Lord.

verse 11

Now you have the facts, and you must apply them. Our old man was crucified. God did that. But you must reckon yourself dead with Jesus by faith. *You* must do that. Until you do, you will continue to be the slave of your old man.

Imagine the worst sort of man—the kind churchgoers cannot abide. He curses, he drinks whiskey, he smokes cigars, he is unkind to his wife and children. Then this man's wife and children become Christians. On Sunday evening they slip out to the local gospel service. As they go out, they see him sitting in his recliner chair with a cigar in his mouth and a bottle of whiskey on the table beside him, watching videos he should not watch. He swears at them as they go past.

They enjoy a wonderful evening at church and come home singing choruses. They walk into the front door expecting him to swear at them. He does not swear. Smoke is curling from the cigar in the ashtray, but he is not smoking. Whiskey remains in the bottle, but he is not drinking. He is not even watching the video playing on TV. Why not? Because he had a heart attack while they were gone and he died. Now he is dead to whiskey. Dead to cigars. Dead to swearing. Dead to the videos. Sin has no more attraction for him. Sin produces no more reaction from him. He is dead.

We have seen the admonition of Romans 6:11: "Reckon yourselves to be dead indeed to sin." What does that mean? That sin has no more attraction for you. Sin produces no more reaction from you. Sin has no more power over you.

How does this take place? By faith in what Jesus did on the cross. Our old man, that criminal, was executed.

God's Remedy for Corruption

At Easter time many years ago, in the days when I was holding open-air street meetings and preaching three times a week in London, I had a vivid dream. In it I saw a man preaching on the street in the very same way that I did. He was doing a good job, and a crowd of people stood around him. This man had a club foot, however, and there was something twisted and crooked about him.

I wonder who that man is, I said to myself.

Two weeks later I had precisely the same dream.

God must be trying to tell me something, I thought to myself. Again I wondered who that man was. His preaching was all right, but there was something crooked about him.

As I was wondering, God said to me what Nathan said to David in 2 Samuel 12:7: "You are the man!"

God was exposing to me the old man inside me. He was still there, I realized, even though I had already been saved and was in the ministry. So I began to study the Scripture, and saw that the remedy for that twisted nature was crucifixion.

Because it was the Easter season, I had a mental picture of three crosses on the hill of Golgotha. The middle cross was taller than the other two. As I meditated on this, the Holy Spirit said to me, *Now tell Me, for whom was the middle cross made? Think before you answer.*

I thought for a moment. "It was made for Barabbas."

That's right. At the last moment, though, Jesus took the place of Barabbas.

"Yes, He did."

But I thought Jesus took your place.
"Yes, that's right!"
Then you must be Barabbas.
At that moment I saw it. I was the criminal for whom the cross was constructed. It fitted me exactly; it was made to my measurements. But Jesus took my place. My old man was crucified in Him. Incredible—but true!

Look at the picture of the old and new man in Ephesians 4:22–24, where Paul exhorts his readers to

put off, concerning your former conduct, the old man which grows corrupt according to the deceitful lusts, and be renewed in the spirit of your mind, and that you put on the new man which was created according to God, in true righteousness and holiness.

Notice Paul is talking to people who are already saved, but he is telling them to put off the old man and put on the new. That is not something that happens when we are saved; it is something we need to do *after* we are saved.

Paul is saying that the old man is experiencing *progressive* corruption because of the lusts of deception that are in it. But the new man, according to Paul, was created "in true righteousness and holiness." A better translation might be: "The new man was created according to God's pattern in righteousness and holiness of the truth"—that is, holiness that proceeds out of the truth. We can receive it only when we have acknowledged the truth about ourselves—that is, the real nature of the old man in us.

In every human life there are two opposing forces at work: *deception* and *truth*. The old man is the product of the devil's deception. Adam and Eve believed his lie: "You will not die; you will be like God." When they opened themselves up to Satan's deception, it produced corruption within them. The key word to describe the old man, therefore, is *corrupt.*

The new man, by contrast, is created afresh by God—a new creation in Christ. It is the product of the truth of God's Word, which produces righteousness and holiness. God's remedy for corruption, then, is to crucify the old man that is the product of deception and to create in us a new man that is the product of the truth.

Notice the difference between the devil's lie and God's truth. God's truth, through the new creation, produces in us righteousness and holiness. On the other hand, the product of the devil's lie—the old man—is absolutely corrupt morally, physically and emotionally.

God showed me years ago that corruption is irreversible. Once it is present, you can slow it down, but there is no way to turn it back. Take, for instance, a beautiful piece of fruit like a peach. It looks perfect but there is corruption at work in it. If you leave it on the kitchen counter for a week, it becomes yellow, shriveled and unattractive. Why? Corruption was in it. The modern solution is to put that peach, when ripe, into the refrigerator. Yet the refrigerator does not reverse corruption; it merely slows it down.

Many churches are like the refrigerator. They do not change corruption; they just slow it down. The only way to change a person is to make him or her a new creation.

God does not patch up or reform the old man. He does not improve or educate him. He puts him to death. In his place comes forth a new creation that is the product of God's truth. "If anyone is in Christ, he is a new creation" (2 Corinthians 5:17).

The Nature of the New Creation

To close our analysis of the new man in exchange for the old man, let's look briefly at the nature of the new creation. The apostle Peter is writing to born-again Christians:

> [You have] been born again, not of corruptible seed but incorruptible, through the word of God which lives and abides forever.
>
> 1 Peter 1:23

The nature of the seed determines the nature of the life that comes out of it. If you sow an orange seed, you do not get an apple. If you sow an apple seed, you do not get an orange. If you are born as a natural person of corruptible seed, you will have a corruptible life—a life subject to the process of corruption. If you are born again of incorruptible seed, however, you will enjoy incorruptible life, because it is impossible for incorruptible seed to produce a corruptible life. The key word describing the new nature is *incorruptible*.

What is the seed that brings forth the new man, and what causes it to be incorruptible? It is the seed of God's Word, which produces incorruptible life.

Look at James 1:18: "Of His own will He brought us forth [or begot us again] by the word of truth." Notice that the new man is the product of the truth. The truth of God's Word begets in us an incorruptible nature.

What does this mean regarding our tendency to sin? First John 3:9 says: "Whoever has been born of God does not sin, for His seed remains in him; and he cannot sin, because he has been born of God."

Derek Prince was born of God about 59 years ago at this writing. Does that mean Derek Prince never sinned after salvation? I can tell you for sure that it does not! Yet the verse says he *cannot* sin. My conclusion is that John is talking not about the individual but about the new man in the individual. Because he is born of incorruptible seed, the new man is incapable of sinning.

I love 1 John 5:4: "Whatever is born of God overcomes the world." It is both a *whoever* and a *whatever*. The apostle John is not talking about James or Bill or George or Mary or Jane. He is talking about the new man produced in us by the Word of God. Again, incorruptible seed produces an incorruptible nature. Does that mean that once we are born again, we can never sin? No. It all depends on which nature is allowed to control us. The old man cannot help sinning. The new man cannot sin. What you do depends on who is in control of you.

A person who has never been born again cannot help sinning, because his very nature causes him to sin. But a person who has been born again has an option. If we allow the new nature to remain in control, we do not sin. If we allow the old nature to reassert itself, we sin.

Claiming This Exchange

Whatever you do, do not try to make the old man behave in a religious way! This does not work. Instead, God's solution is this:

> My old man—the rebel, the corrupt one—was crucified in Jesus that I might be delivered from that evil and corrupt nature, and that a new nature might come into me, through the Word of God, and take control of me.

In the next four chapters we will examine what the cross is designed to do *in* us. Whether we sin or do not sin, whether we have victory or defeat, depends on the measure in which we allow the cross to do its work in us.

Questions for the Study

1. What is our old man?
2. What is God's remedy for our old man?
3. How do we make the crucifixion of our old man effective in our lives?
4. What does it mean to "reckon ourselves to be dead indeed to sin"?
5. According to Ephesians 4:22–24, what are the differences between the old man and the new man?
6. Describe the nature of the new man.
7. Confess with your mouth the exchange given at the end of the chapter.

Part 3

FIVE ASPECTS OF DELIVERANCE

12

DELIVERANCE FROM
THIS PRESENT AGE

In the previous chapters we have been on a journey, discovering what was accomplished for us by the sacrifice of Jesus Christ on the cross. We can summarize our discoveries in the form of these nine divine exchanges as follows:

1. Jesus was punished that I might be forgiven.
2. Jesus was wounded that I might be healed.
3. Jesus was made sin with my sinfulness that I might be made righteous with His righteousness.
4. Jesus died my death that I might share His life.
5. Jesus was made a curse that I might receive the blessing.
6. Jesus endured my poverty that I might share His abundance.
7. Jesus bore my shame that I might share His glory.

8. Jesus endured my rejection that I might have His acceptance.
9. My old man was crucified in Him that the new man might come to life in me.

Now we venture into a new area: what God intends for the cross to do *in* us. This is distinct from what Jesus has done on the cross *for* us. We will never enjoy the permanent benefits of what He has accomplished for us unless we permit the cross to do in us what God has ordained. Nearly all the problems that beset the Church, both collectively and individually, are due to our failure to let the cross do its work in us.

Let's look once again at the problem in the Galatian church: carnality expressed in legalism. Paul was more upset about this problem than he was about the plain, old-fashioned sin in the church at Corinth. That was easier to deal with than this spurious version of Christianity.

Paul's letter to the Galatians was written not as a theological treatise but out of urgency to deal with a real situation. In chapter 7 we noted Paul's warning:

> O foolish Galatians! Who has bewitched you . . . before whose eyes Jesus Christ was clearly portrayed among you as crucified?
>
> Galatians 3:1

The Spirit-filled Galatian Christians had been bewitched. What had witchcraft done? It had obscured the vision of Jesus Christ crucified, which is the only basis of all God's provision for us. Once the cross is obscured, we no longer enjoy God's provision.

Satan was also blinding the eyes of the Galatian believers to the crucified Christ as the basis of Satan's total defeat. On the cross Jesus administered to Satan and his kingdom a total, eternal, irreversible defeat. Satan can do nothing about that glorious fact, other than blind the eyes of the Church to it. (He is very eager to do just that!)

What blesses me is that Paul's letter to the Galatians presents not only the problem but also the solution to a church that had lost its vision of the cross.

Galatians unfolds, as I understand it, five successive deliverances that take place when we allow the cross to do its work in us. Again, I am not talking about what Jesus did for us on the cross. Thank God for that!—but do not stop there. There is a work to be done *within* every believer, through the cross, to deal with our root problems. Here are the five deliverances made possible by the cross:

1. Deliverance from this present evil age
2. Deliverance from the law
3. Deliverance from self
4. Deliverance from the flesh
5. Deliverance from the world

We will look at the first deliverance in this chapter and the rest in the balance of this section.

What Do We Know about This Present Age?

A dear sister once gave me a black T-shirt with white printing on it that said, *Be a radical Christian.* Let me encourage you to adopt that attitude as we proceed.

The very first deliverance occurs in Galatians 1:3–4, and it is radical:

Grace to you and peace from God the Father and our Lord Jesus Christ, who gave Himself for our sins, that He might deliver us from this present evil age, according to the will of our God and Father.

Do you realize it is God's purpose that, through the cross, we should be delivered from this present evil age?

Some translations mix up the words *age* and *world*. One Greek word for age is *cosmos*, from which we get such words as *cosmonaut* and *cosmological*. *Cosmos* is a sociological term in the New Testament describing people of a certain category. We will discuss our deliverance from the *cosmos*, this present world system, in chapter 15.

But when Paul talks here about deliverance from the present evil age, he uses the other Greek word for age, *aeon*, meaning an extended period of time, a period of undetermined length. Time in Scripture is measured in ages and generations. Every age contains a certain number of generations. One of the most beautiful phrases in the Bible, *forever and ever*, should actually be translated *to the ages of the ages*. Not merely do we have ages, but eternity consists of ages made up of ages.

I want to point out to you certain facts about this present age to enable you to understand why we need to be delivered from it.

We Do Not Belong to It

We do not belong to this age. We are people from another age. There is much talk today about the New Age movement, but Christians are actually the people of a new age. We live in this age but belong to a future age. If you or I are living as though we belong forever in this age, we have missed the whole purpose of God.

It Is Coming to a Close

The present age is impermanent and coming to a close. Many passages suggest this.

In Matthew 13:39, for example, speaking about the weeds sown among the wheat, Jesus said, "The enemy who sowed them is the devil, the harvest is the end of the age, and the reapers are the angels." In verse 40 of the same chapter, Jesus said, "So it will be at the end of this age." Again in verse 49: "So it will be at the end of the age."

Many other passages indicate that this age is coming to an end. If you feel as I do about this age, you will say, "Thank God!" I can think of no worse prospect than the present age continuing forever with all its misery, sickness, darkness, ignorance, cruelty and war. Thank God it is not going on forever!

It Has an Evil God

In 2 Corinthians 4:3–4 Paul talks about people who cannot see the Gospel: "Even if our gospel is veiled, it is veiled to those who are perishing, whose minds the god of this age has blinded." Who is the god of this age? Satan. Why is the age evil? Very simply, because it has an evil god.

We know God could depose Satan, but that is not His program. Satan will remain the god of this age so long as this age continues. God's program is to terminate the age. When the age is terminated, Satan will no longer be a god. He knows that well, which is why he does everything in his power to prevent this present age from coming to an end.

Do you realize that one of the reasons Satan resents the Church is that the Church is God's instrument to bring this age to an end? That is one of our main responsibilities, because this age cannot end until we have done what we have to do. What is that? Here are Christ's marching orders to the Church: "This gospel of the kingdom will be preached in all the world as a witness to all the nations, and then the end will come" (Matthew 24:14).

Satan is not threatened by politicians, military commanders or academicians, but by those who preach the Gospel of the Kingdom. Satan opposes the preaching of the Gospel of the Kingdom because when that has been accomplished, the age will end and he will no longer be a god. Bible-believing Christians are the people who threaten him.

Getting Caught Up in It Will Make Us Unfruitful

The writer of Hebrews talks about people who have had spiritual experiences and then choose to go back, deny those experiences and deny Jesus Christ. Notice five experiences these people have had:

> It is impossible for those who were once enlightened [experience number one], and have tasted the heavenly gift [experience number two], and have become partakers of the Holy Spirit [experience number three], and have tasted the good word of God [experience number four] and the powers of the age to come [experience number five], if they fall away, to renew them again to repentance.
>
> Hebrews 6:4–6

Many people today—I believe I am one of them—have enjoyed these experiences. Having been enlightened, tasted the heavenly gift and the good Word of God and become partakers of the Holy Spirit, we have tasted the powers of the age to come. One reason God allows this is to spoil our taste for the powers of this age. God wants us to sample something so different and so utterly superior that we are never again enamored of the powers of this age. Unfortunately I do not see this happening with many Christians.

In Matthew 13, the parable of the sower and the seed, Jesus interpreted the different types of soil and the results produced from the seed. In particular He spoke about the one who received the seed among thorns:

> "He who received seed among the thorns is he who hears the word, and the cares of this world and the deceitfulness of riches choke the word, and he becomes unfruitful."
>
> verse 22

Because the word for "world" here is not *cosmos* but *aeon*, the phrase *the cares of this world* is better translated *the worries of this age.* As for the deceitfulness of riches, people think that riches will make them happy. They never do. Some of the unhappiest people in the world are some of the richest. Another deception of riches is that you suppose they will last forever. Yet when you leave this life, you leave them all behind you.

If you are preoccupied with the issues of this age, you will become an unfruitful Christian and the Word of God will not do its work in you. Perhaps you have been saying, "Why don't I see more results? Why don't I get more answers to prayer? Why am I not successful in leading people to the Lord?" Could it be that you are preoccupied with the worries of this age—financial success, prestige, academic recognition, an elegant lifestyle? Preoccupation with these will make you unfruitful.

Are you living as though this age were going to go on forever? It will not. There will be an end of misery, shame, crime and hunger at the coming of the Lord Jesus. Nothing else will end these problems. The Church has had two thousand years to do so and we have made little progress. In fact, there is more misery, more war, more sickness, more poverty and more ignorance in the world today than ever before. Thank God, the Lord is coming back!

Conformed or Transformed?

As a former professional logician and philosopher, I believe that the epistle to the Romans is the most wonderful piece of logic ever penned by a human being. You need never feel intellectually inferior for believing your Bible! No other work on earth can rival it for intellectual accuracy and clarity.

Most commentators agree, moreover, that Romans 1–11 is the doctrinal heart of the Gospel. Yet Paul, having gone through all the theology of Christ's sacrificial death, ends with its practical outworking in life. (Nowhere in the New Testament is theology divorced from living.) So the apostle comes to the point of applying the theology of Romans 1–11:

> I beseech you therefore, brethren, by the mercies of God. . . .
>
> Romans 12:1

What does Paul want you to do after all this wonderful doctrine? Should you be very spiritual, study a lot more or go off to seminary?

> . . . Present your bodies a living sacrifice. . . . And do not be conformed to this world [literally, *age*], but be transformed by the renewing of your mind.
>
> verses 1–2

How down-to-earth the Bible is! Just when we are getting super-spiritual, God says, "I want your body on the altar without reservation. Once you surrender your body, I will renew your mind."

God does not change you from the outside in; He changes you from the inside out. Religion cleans you up on the outside, dresses you in new clothes and tells you not to eat this or drink that. God changes you from the inside. When you think differently, you will live differently. God is not interested in external change that fails to touch the inner nature. And if you want a renewed mind, you must present your body. God renews your mind on no other basis.

"Do not be like the people of this age," Paul is saying. "Do not think the way they think; do not act the way they act. You must have a different set of priorities, and focus not on the temporal but on the eternal."

This does not mean you are impractical, because the people who focus on the eternal, in the light of God's Word, are the most practical people on earth. They are the ones getting results.

In one final, telling Scripture, we see Paul near the end of his ministry—forsaken even by some of his friends, an elderly man sitting in a cold prison cell awaiting an unjust trial and execution. Was that success by this world's standards? Not even by the Church's standards! I am sure Paul must have shed tears as he informed Timothy that his trusted co-worker Demas, who had been with Paul for many years, "has forsaken me, having loved this present world [age]" (2 Timothy 4:10). Paul had relied on Demas—and he had walked out. Why? Because he loved this present age.

You cannot love this present age and be faithful to Jesus Christ. Thank God He has provided, through the cross, a way of deliverance from this present evil age!

Questions for the Study

1. List the nine divine exchanges discussed in the previous chapters.
2. What five areas of deliverance does Paul reveal to us in Galatians that the cross works in us?
3. What are four characteristics of the present evil age?
4. According to Romans 12:1–2, what do we need to do to be delivered from this present evil age?

13

DELIVERANCE FROM
LAW AND SELF

In the last chapter we discussed deliverance from this present evil age. In this chapter we move on to two of the remaining four deliverances Paul mentions. Turning to Galatians 2:19–20 we read of these two deliverances:

> "I through the law died to the law that I might live to God. I have been crucified with Christ; it is no longer I who live, but Christ lives in me; and the life which I now live in the flesh I live by faith in the Son of God, who loved me and gave Himself for me."

The first deliverance here is from the law; the second is from self. These two go very closely together.

Getting Free from the Law

Multitudes of Christians have never understood our need to be delivered from the law. The relationship of the Christian to the law is the most neglected major theme of New Testament theology. Many Christians who talk about being under grace are living in a kind of twilight, halfway between grace and law, not enjoying the benefits of either.

This is a dangerous thing to say, but I have observed that the churches with the word *grace* in their names often contain the people who know the least about grace. In many cases, although we have declared ourselves no longer under the Law of Moses, we have substituted our own silly little religious laws. Paul said the Law of Moses was holy and good, given by God (see Romans 7:12). If that law, given by God, could not perfect us, no other law can. It is silly to expect it.

By the phrases *under the law* or *subject to the law*, we mean "seeking to achieve righteousness with God by observing a system of laws." We do not mean to suggest that we no longer obey any laws. We mean only that *our righteousness before God is not achieved by keeping a set of rules.*

So let's examine the first deliverance. Quoting Paul: *I through the law died to the law.*

The final thing law can do to you is execute you. Once you have been executed, the law has no more claims on you. The glorious fact of the matter is, I was executed in Christ. My old man was crucified with Him. I am no longer subject to the law. I have moved out of the whole area in which the law operates. I am in a new area now.

Paul says, therefore, "I through the law died to the law that I might live to God." In order to live to God, I have to get free from the law. Until I have died to the law, I cannot live for God. That is a breathtaking statement—but exactly what the New Testament says. Look at Romans 6:6–7 again:

> Our old man was crucified with Him [Jesus], that the body of sin might be done away with, that we should no longer be slaves of sin. For he who has died has been freed from sin.

There is no other escape from the slavery of sin (as we have noted) but to escape that old carnal, Adamic nature. A more accurate translation of the final sentence, as I said in chapter 11, is: "He who has died has been justified from sin." In other words, once I have paid the penalty with death, the law has no more demands on me. I am justified, acquitted, clear out of the territory in which the law has demands on me.

Let's look at Galatians 3:10–12, written to people who had experienced grace, been saved, been baptized in the Holy Spirit and witnessed miracles. Even after all this, they decided that in order to become perfect, they must start keeping the law. Paul called them fools. Then he pointed this out:

> As many as are of the works of the law are under the curse; for it is written, *"Cursed is everyone who does not continue in all things which are written in the book of the law, to do them."*

verse 10

Once you commit yourself to keeping the law as a means of achieving righteousness, you must keep the whole law all the time. If you break any point at any time, you come under a curse. That is what the law itself says in Deuteronomy 27:26: "Cursed is the man who does not uphold the words of this law by carrying them out" (NIV).

Then Paul went on:

> But that no one is justified by the law in the sight of
> God is evident, for *"the just shall live by faith."* Yet the
> law is not of faith, but *"the man who does them* [that is,
> who keeps all the commandments all the time] *shall
> live by them."*
>
> Galatians 3:11–12

The simple alternative is stated in Habakkuk 2:4: "The just
shall live by his faith."

We have two options. We can live by the law and, if we
break it, come under a curse. Or we can live by faith, which
is not living by the law. These are mutually exclusive alternatives. You cannot have the best of both worlds. Actually, what
you will experience is the worst of both worlds!

Living by the Law or by Faith?

Am I relying on keeping the law in order to be righteous with God, or am I simply relying on the fact that I
believe in the death and resurrection of Jesus Christ on
my behalf?

We must turn to Romans again for a moment, since Romans provides the theory, and Galatians provides the application for people who have not absorbed the theory:

> Sin shall not have dominion over you, for you are not
> under law but under grace.
>
> Romans 6:14

Surely that is good news! But the implications are startling.
If you are under law, sin will have dominion over you. But

the reason sin does not need to have dominion over you is that you are not under the law but under grace. Once again these are mutually exclusive alternatives. You may be under law or under grace, but not under both.

We see the same mutually exclusive alternatives in Romans 7:6:

> Now we have been delivered from the law, having died to what we were held by, so that we should serve in the newness of the Spirit and not in the oldness of the letter.

Notice that Paul does not say here that we are delivered from sin or Satan, but from the law. Where did we die? On the cross. When Jesus died, He died in our place. But if we have not been delivered by death from the law, we cannot serve in the newness of the Spirit.

To illustrate the point, imagine planning a trip to an unknown destination. You have two options: You can take a map or you can ask for a personal guide. The map is perfect; it is absolutely accurate. On the other hand, the guide already knows the way. He does not need to consult the map. The map is like the law. But no one has yet arrived at the destination of righteousness by following the map of the law, although millions have tried. Statistics are against you! On the other hand, the Holy Spirit offers Himself as your personal Guide to lead you to your destination.

Which will you choose? Will you take the map, stumble along and end up falling over a precipice onto the dead bodies of millions who have tried before you? Or will you ask the Holy Spirit to lead you?

The Holy Spirit already knows the way; He does not need the map. In fact, it was He who made the map!

Being Led by the Spirit

If you are to be led by the Holy Spirit, you must be sensitive to Him and cultivate a relationship with Him. Let us look at just two Scriptures. First:

> As many as are led by the Spirit of God, these are sons of God.
>
> Romans 8:14

Because the verb tense of *are led* is the continuing present, the verse might be better translated, "As many as are regularly led by the Spirit of God, these are sons of God."

The Greek word for *sons* refers not to babies but to mature sons. When you are born again of the Holy Spirit, you are a spiritual infant. There is only one pathway to growth from infancy to maturity: to be led by the Holy Spirit. What must you do to become a mature son of God? Be led by the Holy Spirit. We know from the limiting clause indicating *as many as* that there is no other way.

The second Scripture is Galatians 5:18:

> If you are led [again, *regularly led*] by the Spirit, you are not under the law.

Did you catch that? We have just seen that the only way to spiritual maturity is to be led by the Spirit. Now we see that if you are regularly led by the Spirit, and thus become mature, then you are not under the law. You cannot mix the law and the Spirit. You must make a breathtaking decision—one that is frightening. I will no longer rely on a set of rules to make me righteous. I will simply trust the Holy Spirit to lead me.

But then comes the agonizing question: If I stop keeping rules, what will happen? Will I do the wrong thing? Let me reassure you, the Holy Spirit will never lead you to do anything wrong. Can you trust Him? It is your security!

Letting Jesus Take Charge

Before we move on to deal with the second deliverance, let me reiterate that there are only two ways of achieving righteousness: by works and by grace. One is law, the other faith. One is keeping rules, the other is being led by the Holy Spirit.

Did you know that Orthodox Judaism has 613 commandments? Most Orthodox Jews will confess (not in public but in private) that they keep only 32. But God's way of righteousness is not struggling; it is yielding. To whom do I yield? I yield through the Holy Spirit to Jesus in me. Jesus is my righteousness, my wisdom, my holiness, my redemption.

I recall the story of a woman greatly admired for her personal holiness. Somebody asked her one day, "Sister, what do you do when you're tempted?"

"When the devil knocks at the door," she replied, "I let Jesus answer."

Success is not found, you see, in meeting the devil in your own strength, but in letting Jesus move in and take charge of the situation. It is not struggling; it is yielding. Not effort but union. Jesus said, "I am the vine, you are the branches" (John 15:5). Do vines bear grapes by keeping rules? You can dangle all the rules for bearing fruit in front of a vine, but it will not bother to look at them. A vine branch yields grapes because the life of the vine is flowing into the branch.

In this simple picture, we could say that the vine stock represents Jesus and the sap that flows out from this through the branches is the Holy Spirit.

If we let ourselves get severed from Jesus, we are in trouble. But as long as we abide in Him, we are all right.

Dying to Ourselves

The second deliverance is found, once again, in Galatians 2:20:

> I have been crucified with Christ; it is no longer I who live, but Christ lives in me.

The deliverance here can be expressed in four short words: "Not I, but Christ." We must be delivered from self.

Self will never cease its important demands: "I'm important. Look at me. Help me. Pray for me. Heal me. I need help now." Self-centered people with problems become the slaves of their problems. The more they focus on themselves and their problems, the more self-centered they become, and the more enslaved to self.

The alternative is Christ: "Not I, but Christ." That is a decision you have to make: "I abdicate. In my place I let Jesus move in and take over." Many people are trying to follow the Lord but have never taken that first step.

It is stated plainly in Matthew 16:24:

> Jesus said to His disciples, "If anyone desires to come after Me [follow Me, live like Me], let him deny himself, and take up his cross, and follow Me."

You cannot follow Jesus until you have done those two things: denied yourself and taken up your cross.

What does it mean to deny yourself? The word *deny* means to say no. To deny yourself is to say no to yourself. Self says, "I want," and then you say, "No." Self says, "I feel," and you say, "What you feel is not what matters; it is what God says." You have to turn against that self in you.

Next, you must take up your cross. I have heard two good definitions of *cross*. First, the cross is the place where your will and God's will cross. Second, the cross is the place where you die. God will not put the cross on you. You must take it up of your own free will.

Jesus said, on His way to the cross, "No one takes [My life] from Me, but I lay it down of Myself" (John 10:18). That is also true of you when you follow Jesus. No one can take your life from you. The preacher cannot do it; the Church cannot do it. Only you can decide to take up your cross and die on it. When Christ died, you died: "I am crucified with Christ." That is the end of your ego. Only then can you follow Jesus.

The Self-Humbling of Jesus

A tremendous passage of Scripture paints a picture of what is involved practically in this exchange:

> Let this mind be in you which was also in Christ Jesus, who, being in the form of God, did not consider it robbery to be equal with God, but made Himself of no reputation, taking the form of a bondservant, and coming in the likeness of men. And being found in appearance as a man, He humbled Himself and became obedient to the point of death, even the death of the cross.
>
> Philippians 2:5–8

In the last two verses of that passage, Paul describes the self-humbling of Jesus through seven steps downward that He took to His death on the cross:

Step #1: "[He] made Himself of no reputation." The Greek says, "He emptied Himself." Charles Wesley wrote that He "emptied Himself of all but love."

Step #2: He took "the form of a bondservant." He could still have been an angel and been a servant—but He had to go further downward.

Step #3: He came "in the likeness of men." He took on human nature.

Step #4: He was "found in appearance as a man." I understand this to mean that when He appeared on the streets of Nazareth, nothing distinguished Him from the other men and women around Him.

Step #5: "He humbled Himself." Not merely was He a man; He was a humble man. Not a priest, not a ruler—a carpenter.

Step #6: He "became obedient to . . . death." He not only lived as a man; He died as a man.

Step #7: He died the ultimate death—"the death of the cross."

God's Exaltation of Jesus

The next three verses of Philippians 2 describe the seven-fold exaltation of Jesus:

Therefore God also has highly exalted Him and given Him the name which is above every name, that at the name of Jesus every knee should bow, of those in heaven, and of those on earth, and of those under the earth, and that every tongue should confess that Jesus Christ is Lord, to the glory of God the Father.

verses 9–11

Notice the *therefore* at the beginning. Why did God exalt Jesus? Because He humbled Himself. Jesus said that "he who humbles himself will be exalted" (Matthew 23:12). It is the guaranteed way to exaltation. God has taken responsibility for the consequences. The lower down you go, the higher up you will end. Your part of the process is going down; God's part is raising you up.

Now here are the seven upward stages of the exaltation of Jesus:

Stage #1: God "highly exalted Him."
Stage #2: God "[gave] Him the name which is above every name."
Stage #3: At the name of Jesus every knee will bow.
Stage #4: Everything in heaven will bow.
Stage #5: Everything on earth will bow.
Stage #6: Everything under the earth will bow.
Stage #7: Every tongue will "confess that Jesus Christ is Lord, to the glory of God the Father."

Notice the perfect parallel structure of the verses in this passage. Did Paul sit in his cell and plan some elaborate composition? No, he was inspired by the Holy Spirit!

The Way Up Is Down

Although Christ "did not consider equality with God something to be grasped" (Philippians 2:6, NIV), another person *did* consider equality with God something to be grasped.

Lucifer reached up, slipped and fell. Jesus stooped down and was raised up.

The American evangelist D. L. Moody once said, "As a young preacher I used to think God kept His gifts on shelves. The best gifts were on the highest shelves and I had to reach up for them. Later I discovered that the best gifts were on the lowest shelves and I had to stoop down for them."

The lesson for us is this: *The way up is down.* The way to life is death. If you want to go up, go down. Not I, but Christ. It is a decision. God has made the decision possible, but you have to make the decision personally.

To see the practical outworking of this concept, let's go back to the verses that immediately precede this great passage:

> Let nothing be done through selfish ambition or conceit, but in lowliness of mind let each esteem others better than himself. Let each of you look out not only for his own interests, but also for the interests of others.
>
> Philippians 2:3–4

I said in the last chapter that nearly all the problems that beset the Church, both collectively and individually, are due to our failure to let the cross do its work in us. I also believe that most of the problems in the Church, and particularly in the ministry—for example, as Paul says here, selfish ambition and conceit—are traceable to one cause. Rebellion is a root of many personal problems, but there is a "root to the root": *pride.* Pride is what releases the other problems.

If you trace the history of sin in the universe, it began not on earth but in heaven. The first sin was the pride of Lucifer, which led to his rebellion. Anyone who is proud will end up a rebel. That is the final outcome of self-centeredness.

I meet people who are running away from their problems. Sometimes they are willing to travel around the earth to get away from their problems. But the truth is, wherever you go, you take your biggest problem with you: yourself! The only solution is the cross. A beautiful Scripture sums it all up:

> To [the saints] God willed to make known what are the riches of the glory of this mystery among the Gentiles: which is Christ in you, the hope of glory.
>
> Colossians 1:27

There is the secret: *Christ in you.* When does that become real in your life? When you experience deliverance from self; when you say, "Not I, but Christ."

Questions for the Study

1. What has to happen in order that we can live to God?
2. According to Habakkuk 2:4, what do we live by?
3. Romans 6:14 says that we are under what?
4. How do we become spiritually mature?
5. What four words describe being delivered from self?
6. What two things must you do to follow Jesus?
7. What does it mean to deny yourself?
8. What does it mean to take up your cross?
9. What is the lesson we learn from Jesus in Philippians 2:5–8?

14

DELIVERANCE FROM THE FLESH

We are looking at five different deliverances listed in Galatians, which God offers us through the work of the cross within us. Having looked at three so far, we will recapitulate them.

First, Galatians 1:4 says God has delivered us from this present evil age. Next, Galatians 2:19 says God has delivered us from the law. Finally, Galatians 2:20 says we can be delivered from self.

Wonderful! Now we go on to the fourth deliverance, found in Galatians 5:24:

Those who are Christ's have crucified the flesh with its passions and desires.

Consider for a moment what deliverance from the flesh means. It does not mean we are delivered out of our physical bodies. *The flesh* can be interpreted, rather, as the way the old man expresses itself in and through us. We have already spoken about the old man—the rebellious nature that each one of us has inherited by descent from Adam. *The flesh* and *the old man* are closely tied together.

Since this verse says that "those who are Christ's have crucified the flesh," we have a distinguishing mark of those who belong to Christ. In 1 Corinthians 15:23, speaking of the order in which the dead are to be resurrected, Paul uses the same phrase:

> But each one in his own order: Christ the firstfruits [who has already been resurrected], afterward *those who are Christ's* at His coming.
>
> emphasis added

Christ is coming back as a thief, in the sense that He will return at an unexpected moment; but there the likeness ends. He will take only those who belong to Him.

Returning to Galatians 5:24, we discover the kind of persons for whom Jesus is coming: those who "have crucified the flesh with its passions and desires."

Belonging to Christ, then, is not a denominational matter. Jesus is coming back not specifically for Protestants or Catholics or Baptists or Pentecostals, but for people who fulfill a particular condition: They have crucified their flesh with its passions and desires.

Four Works of the Flesh

Earlier in Galatians 5 Paul gives us a list of the works of the flesh—the way the fleshly nature expresses itself in our lives. "The works of the flesh," Paul says, "are evident" (verse 19). All too evident, I would say. Not always evident to the one who practices them, but evident to everyone else. These works are

> adultery, fornication, uncleanness, lewdness, idolatry, sorcery, hatred, contentions, jealousies, outbursts of wrath, selfish ambitions, dissensions, heresies, envy, murders, drunkenness, revelries, and the like; of which I tell you beforehand, just as I also told you in time past, that those who practice such things will not inherit the kingdom of God.
>
> verses 19–21

You can search in vain for anything good in this list. Nothing good ever comes out of the flesh. It is incapable of producing good. It is clear that you cannot live according to the flesh and inherit the Kingdom of God. They are mutually exclusive.

Remember the key word that describes the old nature: *corrupt*. Anything the flesh produces is corrupt. It cannot produce anything good.

There are four main categories of the works of the flesh.

Sexual Impurity

Sexual impurity includes fornication or sexual immorality, uncleanness and lewdness. Fornication—or sexual immorality—covers every kind of sexual immorality: premarital sex (if you want to give it that fancy name); adultery (the breaking of a marriage covenant); homosexuality; and every other type of perversion.

Churches or denominations ordain whom they will. But that does not change what the Bible says: Those who practice sexual impurity are excluded from the Kingdom of God.

The Occult

The second category of the works of the flesh is the occult: idolatry and sorcery. An alternative translation for *sorcery* is witchcraft. Initially witchcraft, though a satanic activity, is a work of the flesh. Its objective is to manipulate and control. Once the flesh comes into operation, however, the satanic moves in and takes over.

Recall that the first desire of Adam and Eve that led them into trouble was *to know*. That is a desire of the flesh. Uncounted millions are captivated by the occult because they want to find out things God has not permitted them to know. Going to a fortuneteller is motivated by the fleshly desire to know—a work of the flesh. The same applies to consulting the horoscope.

Sometimes people are inclined to plead ignorance as an excuse, saying, "I didn't know there was anything wrong with that." But ignorance is no excuse. In 1 Timothy 1:13–15 Paul acknowledges that he was the chief of sinners for things he did "ignorantly in unbelief."

The word translated *sorcery* is directly related to the Greek word for drugs—the same word from which we get *pharmacy*. The cult of drugs is sorcery. Those who engage in it are outside the Kingdom of God.

Division

The third and longest part of Paul's list, very little attended to, centers around division. Paul identifies "hatred, contentions, jealousies, outbursts of wrath, selfish ambitions, dissensions, heresies, envy." Every broken personal relationship, everything that divides homes and families, and every kind of division in the Body of Christ, is a product of the flesh.

Self-Indulgence

The fourth and final category is "drunkenness, revelries, and the like." I understand this to refer to unrestrained indulgence of fleshly appetites and desires, especially in the area of food and drink. In 1 Corinthians 9:27 Paul describes the kind of discipline in this area that he imposed on himself:

> I discipline my body and bring it into subjection, lest, when I have preached to others, I myself should become disqualified.

If we decide to follow Paul's example, we can invoke the help of the Holy Spirit, whom Paul describes as "a spirit of power, of love and of *self-discipline*" (2 Timothy 1:7, NIV, emphasis added). But if we continue to be undisciplined and self-indulgent, the Holy Spirit will not impose on us a discipline that is contrary to the lifestyle of our choice.

The Enemy Within

Some theologians have said that in 1 Corinthians 3:3, Paul called the Corinthian Christians carnal because they spoke so much in tongues. The problem in Corinth was not speaking in tongues, however, but wrong attitudes and relationships that revealed carnality—the work of the flesh. What is the mark of carnality?

> Where there are envy, strife, and divisions among you, are you not carnal and behaving like mere men? For when one says, "I am of Paul," and another, "I am of Apollos," are you not carnal?
>
> 1 Corinthians 3:3–4

It is not theology that divides the church. People can use theology in a very carnal way, but it is carnality, not theology, that is the root of the problem. Carnality is division, following human leaders. One says, "I follow Luther"; another says, "I follow Calvin"; another says, "I follow Wesley." You can receive the teaching of those men and thank God for it. But becoming a follower of one leader or another marks you as carnal.

There is only one solution to this, as well as to every kind of carnality: the cross. Where people are unwilling to submit to the cross in their lives, there will be division, strife, envy, jealousy and pride.

But let me say something here that I hope will help you, lest you form the impression, "I am not up to standard. I have not arrived at the place you're describing." Relax! God does not expect you to have arrived. He trusts that you are on the way. We need to realize that every one of us has an enemy of God within us. Most of our struggles and difficulties as Christians are due to this enemy within.

If you lived through World War II, you are familiar with the idea of *the fifth column.* The phrase came originally from the Spanish Civil War in the 1930s, when Spaniards were fighting Spaniards inside Spain. The story goes that when a certain Spanish general was besieging Madrid in 1936, another general came to him and asked, "What is your plan to capture the city?"

"I have four columns advancing against the city," he replied, "one from the north, one from the east, one from the south and one from the west." Then he paused and added, "But it's my fifth column that I expect to take the city for me."

"Where is your fifth column?" asked the second general.

"Inside the city," came the reply.

That is our problem. The Church is never defeated from without. The Church is undefeatable except by the fifth column—the enemy inside.

Reckoning Our Flesh to Be Dead

Every one of us has a similar enemy inside. It is the flesh. So do not feel guilty if you are struggling inside. That may mean you are more alive than Christians who have no struggles. The enemy is not meeting with any opposition within them. Look at what Paul says in Romans 7:18:

> I know that in me (that is, in my flesh) nothing good dwells; for to will is present with me, but how to perform what is good I do not find.

Sometimes I say that the difference between the apostle Paul and most of us was what he knew that we do not know. He said, "I know there is nothing good in my fleshly nature. Therefore I cannot expect any good to come out of it. No matter how hard I want to do what is good, I am faced with a continual struggle with something inside me that does not want to do what is good."

The struggle itself is, in a sense, a good sign. It is a sign that you are alive. Let me tell you, Paul was not an immature Christian when he wrote Romans 7! He was on the threshold of Romans 8. But you never really get into Romans 8 until you have learned to deal with your flesh.

We must move on, then, to Romans 8:6–7:

> For to be carnally minded is death, but to be spiritually minded is life and peace. Because the carnal mind is enmity against God; for it is not subject to the law of God, nor indeed can be.

To let your fleshly nature control your thinking is death, but to let the Holy Spirit control the way you think produces life and peace. There is no way to bring your fleshly nature into obedience to God. It will never obey God. Accept that fact. Don't try to make it obey God. Don't try to make it religious. Don't try to take it to church, and sit for hours in meetings and go through a lot of religious exercises trying to make it obey God. It will not obey; it cannot do so. It is incurably corrupt, a rebel to the roots.

What is the remedy? God's solution is execution. The good news is, the execution took place more than nineteen centuries ago. When Jesus died on the cross, our old man, that carnal nature, was put to death in Him. What we have to do is simply apply what Jesus accomplished for us on the cross:

> Knowing this, that our old man was crucified with Him [Jesus], that the body of sin might be done away with, that we should no longer be slaves of sin.
>
> Romans 6:6

This is a historical fact—true whether we know it or not, whether we believe it or not. When we know it and believe it, however, it works in us. Again I have to point out a problem with much of the contemporary Church: Most Christians do not know they were crucified with Christ.

Actually to say that the old man has been *done away with* is misleading. As long as we are in this life, we never come to the end of our carnal nature. I have met people who believe they were totally delivered from the flesh, but I did not see the evidence. They merely changed their terminology. They no longer lost their tempers; they indulged in "righteous indignation." As I understand it, the flesh can be rendered ineffective, incapable of doing what it would like to do; but in this age it cannot be eliminated. This is another reason to look for another age!

Three Simple Words

In Romans 6:11 Paul says:

Likewise you also, reckon yourselves to be dead indeed to sin.

Notice the progression. In verse 6, which we just looked at, we are to *know* we are dead to sin, but in verse 11 we *reckon* it, or apply it to ourselves. I do that when I say, "My carnal nature has been crucified."

Three simple words may help you in this reckoning process: *fact, faith, feeling.* Notice the order. You do not begin with your feelings. You begin with the facts, which are the truths of the Bible. The Bible contains truth, or facts, and your faith is built on the facts; then your feelings come into line with your faith. Never let your feelings dictate to you.

What I am bringing forth in these chapters is fact. Perhaps it seems a little too objective or remote to you, but the truth is, we must begin with the objective. If we begin with our feelings, we are without an anchor, at the mercy of every wind or current. So we begin with the scriptural facts, basing our faith on them and allowing our feelings to come into line.

Sometimes when you or I feel like the most miserable failures, we are actually more pleasing to God than when we think we are doing tremendously. God is near those who are of a broken heart. In fact, "the sacrifices of God *are* a broken spirit" (Psalm 51:17, emphasis added). One trait that keeps God at a distance is self-confidence.

I have encountered problems that I said I could handle, and later on wished I had never said that! Years ago my first wife, Lydia, and I took our first journey to the United States from Canada. I had heard things about America that made me nervous. There were freeways on which you could not drive less than forty miles an hour, and that frightened me! So we planned our route from Oshawa south to Lima, New York, to avoid all freeways.

After a safe trip into New York State, we were starting back to Canada when Lydia said, "I think we should pray."

"There's no need to pray," I said.

We got onto the New York State Thruway and set out confidently. But because the exit signs on major roadways in the United States are different from those in Canada, we passed the correct exit, only to learn that the next exit was 57 miles farther on. We had to drive 114 miles out of our way. Then, when we got off at the right exit, the car broke down.

I will not tell you the rest of the story, except to add that I have never again said there is no need to pray!

So How Do We Crucify the Flesh?

As we seek deliverance from the flesh, there is an important word of warning in 1 Peter 4:1–2:

> Therefore, since Christ suffered for us in the flesh, arm yourselves also with the same mind, for he who has suffered in the flesh has ceased from sin, that he no longer should live the rest of his time in the flesh for the lusts of men, but for the will of God.

Peter warns us that deliverance from the flesh will not come without suffering. We must arm ourselves with this expectation, therefore, and be ready to embrace whatever it takes to be free from the domination of our fleshly nature. This kind of mental armor is essential for victory, but far too many Christians face their tests without it. They are not mentally prepared for the pressures and conflicts that await them. All too often, therefore, they allow their fleshly nature to defeat them.

For years I had a hard time understanding the statement that "he who has suffered in the flesh has ceased from sin." I said to myself, *I thought all the suffering took place when Jesus died on the cross. I can't add anything to what He has already suffered.*

Eventually, however, I saw that the suffering lies in crucifying our flesh. Remember what we said at the beginning of this chapter? "Those who are Christ's have crucified the flesh with its passions and desires." It is not painless for any one of us to crucify our flesh. It means, in a certain sense, that we must stretch ourselves out on the cross and drive the nails into our own hands and feet.

Here is an example of crucifying the flesh. Let's say that a young woman in her early twenties, a committed Christian eager to serve the Lord, meets a young man. He claims to be a Christian and goes to church, but only to be with this young woman. He says he wants to marry her. She has become emotionally involved with him and does not know what to do.

Then her godly pastor, who has gotten to know the young man and who cares for her soul, tells her, "He's not a real Christian; he's just putting on an act because he wants you. Please don't marry him."

She has two options. She can gratify her flesh or crucify it. Her flesh says, "But I love him." Then she says, "But I love Jesus more." She drives the first nail into her right hand. Again the voice of her flesh: "But I want a home and children." She drives the second nail into her left hand. The same voice: "But I'm afraid of being lonely for the rest of my life." She drives the final nail into her feet.

Do you understand? Both the hands and the feet must be nailed. It is painful, but the pain does not last long. After a while she is free and happy—and in due course the right man comes along.

But suppose she refuses to crucify her flesh. She marries the man and soon realizes that he does not really love the Lord and that he will not be any kind of spiritual head or help to her. Then, after fifteen years of strife, he deserts her, leaving her with three children.

Which is more painful—dealing with her flesh or spending fifteen years married to the wrong man and then being left alone with the children? To be sure, it is painful either way. But the root cause of our pain is our fleshly nature. The question is, will you accept God's solution or go the other way? God's solution is painful, but only temporarily. Her broken heart will mend after a year or two; then she is free to live the rest of her life for God.

A crisis comes in the lives of most Christians, I believe, especially those called to some special field of ministry. In this crisis they either do what the flesh wants, and miss God, or else they crucify the flesh and suffer. Out of the suffering comes a developed character and a committed life that is no longer enslaved to sin.

I can see a point, looking back on my own experience, when I was faced with making either the right decision or the wrong decision. I could go the way of my flesh, please myself and take the easy course; or else I could apply the cross. Rather clumsily, not really understanding what I was doing, I drove in the nails. More than fifty years later, I am glad I did!

Carefully reread what Peter says in this passage: "Therefore, since Christ suffered for us in the flesh, arm yourselves also with the same mind, for he who has suffered in the flesh has ceased from sin, that he no longer should live the rest of his time in the flesh for the lusts of men, but for the will of God."

Isn't that tremendous? You can come to the place where sin no longer dominates you! This is the fourth glorious deliverance that is provided by the cross.

Questions for the Study

1. What is meant by the term *the flesh*?
2. What kind of people belong to Jesus?
3. List the four categories of the works of the flesh.
4. What three words help us reckon ourselves to be dead?
5. How do we crucify the flesh?

15

DELIVERANCE FROM THE WORLD

One final deliverance remains. It is articulated in Galatians 6:14, where Paul was writing about people who wanted to boast in certain religious accomplishments:

> God forbid that I should boast except in the cross of our Lord Jesus Christ, by whom the world has been crucified to me, and I to the world.

The cross comes between the true Christian and the world. The world looking in the direction of the Christian sees a corpse on a cross, which is not attractive. The Christian looking in the direction of the world sees something similar. There is nothing to attract him, and there is a complete line of separation between the two, marked out by the cross.

We must consider again what is meant by *the world*. Remember from chapter 12 the two words for *age* that are sometimes confused: *aeon* and *cosmos*. *Aeon* is a measure of time, while *cosmos* (or *world*) is sociological, dealing with people. The word in Galatians 6:14 for *world* is *cosmos*. We are delivered from this present world system, consisting of all those who refuse the righteous government of God in the Person of Jesus Christ.

A revealing parable appears in Luke 19. Jesus said:

> "A certain nobleman went into a far country to receive for himself a kingdom and to return. So he called ten of his servants, delivered to them ten minas, and said to them, 'Do business till I come.' But his citizens hated him, and sent a delegation after him, saying, 'We will not have this man to reign over us.'"
>
> verses 12–14

Here is a picture of Jesus leaving this earth, going to His Father in heaven and then waiting to come back to take His Kingdom. But it is also a picture of the world system in which people say, "We will not have this Man Jesus to reign over us, nor will we submit to Him as Lord."

What Is the Dividing Line?

The world contains all sorts of people—atheists; people of various religions; respectable, good-living people. You may say of this latter category, "They can't be part of the world. Why, they go to church!" But the way you find out whether people are part of the world system is to challenge them with unreserved commitment to Jesus Christ. Something may rise up in them that is not so respectable. This religious veneer, once removed, will reveal a rebel inside—a religious rebel, perhaps, a good-living rebel, a respectable rebel, but a rebel as much as a Communist is, or an atheist or a Muslim.

What is the dividing line? Submission to Jesus as Lord. Those who are submitted are not in the world. They have passed out of the world and into the Kingdom of God. You cannot be in the Kingdom of God, you see, without a right relationship to the King. Many people want to be in the Kingdom but do not want the King! That was true of Israel in Jesus' time. They wanted the Kingdom but rejected the King; and in rejecting the King they forfeited the Kingdom.

No one can reject the King and be in the Kingdom. What determines whether or not we are in the Kingdom is not the kind of clothes we wear or the kind of entertainment we enjoy; it is our relationship to Jesus. Are we honestly and sincerely submitted to Him? This does not mean we are perfect. In fact, when we submit to Jesus, He usually has a lot of straightening out to do in our lives. It does mean that we continue, sometimes reluctantly, to let Him straighten us out. We may not always enjoy it, but it is better than the alternative!

I was part of this world when the Lord met me. As a professional philosopher I did not care about religion. But one night God yanked me out of the world and dumped me into the Kingdom. I had no doctrinal knowledge, but I had met Jesus and surrendered to Him.

I have had many struggles since then, believe me, but I have never had any desire to go back to the world. What is there in the world? Nothing whatever there attracts or entices me.

It may not always be easy in the Kingdom of God, but it is incomparably better than being in the world! I came out in

one night, like Israel out of Egypt. I have never for one moment wanted to go back. It was not doctrine that changed
me; it was Jesus. I had met Someone who commanded my
loyalty and my obedience.

The World System

In 2 Peter 3:5 Peter speaks about the judgments of God
on the world system:

> For this they [certain people] willfully forget: that by
> the word of God the heavens were of old, and the earth
> standing out of water and in the water, by which the
> world that then existed perished, being flooded with
> water.

When Peter says "the world that then existed perished," he
is not speaking primarily of the physical world that existed
at that time. The earth itself did not perish; the solar system
did not disappear. What perished, on the deepest level, was
a certain sociological order—the order of men before the
flood. What was their problem? They were not submitted to
the righteous government of God. God did away with them
in one brief, comprehensive judgment.

Now a new world order has come into being—different in
many respects, but it has one thing in common with the world
before the flood: It is not submitted to the righteous government of God. But God offers no alternative government; it
is Jesus or nothing.

Let us consider some of what the New Testament tells
us about the world system. These truths are sobering—and
largely ignored in the contemporary Church.

Three Basic Temptations

First John 2:15–16 is contrary to contemporary thinking but is very true:

> Do not love the world or the things in the world. If anyone loves the world, the love of the Father is not in him. For all that is in the world—the lust of the flesh, the lust of the eyes, and the pride of life—is not of the Father but is of the world.

This is perfectly plain, isn't it? There is no theological problem with understanding it. Nothing in the world's motivations, attitudes, ambitions, desires, standards or priorities is of the Father. But we have to be careful in our understanding of this truth. We are not the enemy of sinners. God loved the world and gave His Son for it. We are not to love the world order or the way it lives. We cannot be friends with the world and friends with God. But like Jesus Himself we can be friends of sinners.

This passage reveals the three basic temptations: *the lust of the flesh* (the desires of the physical body), *the lust of the eyes* (the lust of covetousness) and *the pride of life* ("No one tells *me* what to do!"). These temptations were at work in the Garden of Eden. The tree of the knowledge of good and evil was good for food (lust of the flesh) and attractive to the eyes (lust of the eyes), and it could make the man and woman wise without God (pride of life).

Jesus encountered the same three temptations in the wilderness. First, Satan said, "Command that these stones become bread" (Matthew 4:3). That is the lust of the flesh. Next, from the pinnacle of the Temple, "Throw Yourself down" (Matthew 4:6). In other words, "Do something to demonstrate how great You are without the Father." That is the pride of life. And finally, showing Jesus all the kingdoms of the world and their glory: "You can have it all on one condition—just bow down and worship me" (see Matthew 4:9). That represents the lust of the eyes.

Thank God that, while Adam failed in a perfect environment, Jesus, the last Adam, in a desert after forty days without food, was totally victorious.

The temptations Jesus defeated include the nature of all the temptations of the world. Every temptation falls under one of the three headings: the lust of the flesh, the lust of the eyes and, most dangerous of all, the pride of life.

The World Will Not Last

The world is passing away, and the lust of it; but he who does the will of God abides forever.

1 John 2:17

What a breathtaking statement! Everything in the world is impermanent. None of it is going to last. But if you unite your will with the will of God, saying, "I am here to do His will," you are as unshakable and undefeatable as the will of God itself. You will never be defeated, because ultimately God's will can never be defeated. The key is to align your will with His.

The devil will try to convince you that you will have to give up too much. But he is a liar; do not listen to him. It is a *blessed* thing to join your will with God's! It takes away the burden of feeling that "I've got no one to rely on but myself." Roll the burden on the Father; He will take care of you.

We Must Not Be Friends with the World

I think you will agree that James was very plain-spoken:

> Adulterers and adulteresses! Do you not know that friend-
> ship with the world is enmity with God? Whoever there-
> fore wants to be a friend of the world makes himself an
> enemy of God.
>
> James 4:4

Why does he say "adulterers?" Because Christians who
turn to the world after committing themselves to God are
committing spiritual adultery—breaking their betrothal commitment to Jesus. You cannot say it more clearly than that.
Friendship with the world system is enmity with God! You
must choose.

The World Will Hate Us

Of the various writers of the New Testament, John spends
the most time dealing with the world. It is one of his major
themes. In John 15:18–19 he records the words that Jesus
shared with His disciples just before leaving them:

> "If the world hates you, you know that it hated Me before
> it hated you. If you were of the world, the world would
> love its own. Yet because you are not of the world, but
> I chose you out of the world, therefore the world hates
> you."

In the remarkable verse 19, the phrase *the world* occurs
five times. God must be trying to say something! Look at it
again carefully:

"If you were of the world, the world would love its own.
Yet because you are not of the world, but I chose you out
of the world, therefore the world hates you."

There can be no doubt about Jesus' meaning. We should
not be shocked if the world hates us. The problem with the
contemporary Church is, the world does *not* hate us.

Earlier on Jesus said to His brothers who did not believe
in Him, "The world cannot hate you, but it hates Me because I testify of it that its works are evil" (John 7:7). His
brothers were part of the world, because at that time they
had rejected God's righteous government in the Person of
their brother.

As long as you are part of the world, it will not hate you.
But if you are separated from the world and bear witness to
the truth of righteousness, the world *will* hate you. Why does
the world today seldom hate the Church? Because we do not
embarrass it. It feels comfortable with us.

Someone has estimated that there are fifty million born-
again Christians in America. If that were really true, the world
would feel the impact. But the truth is, we Christians scarcely
affect the world. It just shrugs its shoulders. Similarly, in most
European nations today, Christianity is regarded as an anach-
ronism, a remote presence from the past. It has cathedrals
here and there, but nothing much to say to contemporary
life. The world is not against Christianity; the world just
goes its way.

The World Is in Satan's Hands

Do not get angry with me for what follows. Get angry
with John, who wrote it!

> We know that we are of God, and the whole world lies under the sway of the wicked one.
>
> 1 John 5:19

Who is the wicked one? Satan. A more literal translation would be, "The whole world lies *in* the wicked one." In other words, he has the whole world under his control.

Revelation 12:9, another passage penned by John, gives the four main titles of Satan all in one verse:

> The great dragon was cast out, that serpent of old, called the Devil and Satan, who deceives the whole world.

First, our adversary is the *devil*. The Greek word *diabolos* means, literally, "slanderer." Then, he is *Satan*, which means the enemy, the resister, the opposer. Third, he is a *dragon*, a monstrous, frightening creature. Finally, he is the *serpent*, a wily snake. If he cannot force his way in through the front door, he will sneak in through the drain hole!

What does Satan do in these four roles? He deceives the whole world.

The Way Out of the World's System

If you accept all these statements about the world, you must acknowledge that, as committed Christians, we have no place in the world. We simply do not belong in it. The list I gave of the forms that the world's deceptions take is far from complete. We must be delivered from the world's opinions, values, judgments, pressures and enticements. We cannot allow any of those to dictate our thinking.

The greatest single channel of the world's pressure in our contemporary culture is television. I am not saying that all television is wrong, but your TV set channels the world into your home. Television entices and manipulates. It is a demonstration of witchcraft, or spiritual control on a vast scale. Similarly the aim of much TV advertising is to make you want things you do not need and buy things you cannot afford. And it works! Advertisers spend billions of dollars on advertising because they get multiplied billions back.

I do not decide your lifestyle, but I have decided mine, and television does not dominate it. That is not a sacrifice! If you wanted to torment me, you could put me in front of a television set and make me watch it for several hours each day.

I am not suggesting that everyone should be like me. But you need to ask yourself: *Where are my values, standards, judgments and priorities coming from?*

Now let's look for a moment at Paul's melancholy picture in Philippians 3:18–19 of Christians who do not apply the cross in their lives:

> Many walk, of whom I have told you often, and now tell you even weeping, that they are the enemies of the cross of Christ: whose end is destruction, whose god is their belly, and whose glory is in their shame—who set their mind on earthly things.

What is their root problem? They are not enemies of Christ Himself but they are enemies of His cross. They want everything they can get from Jesus. There is just one thing they do not want: the work of His cross in their lives. Notice that their "god is their belly." Doesn't that apply to some of us

Christians? It also says their "glory is in their shame." Some Christians revel in things of which they should be ashamed. The situation is summed up in one phrase: They "set their mind on earthly things."

And the result? They are headed for destruction—a terrible word that applies to time and to eternity. May God help us and deliver us from the system of the world!

Repent

There is only one way out, an old-fashioned word that has dropped out of the religious vocabulary of many of us: *repentance.* Consider the admonition of the forerunner who came to prepare the way for Jesus:

> "Repent, for the kingdom of heaven is at hand!"
>
> Matthew 3:2

Remember God's purpose in the Gospel: to introduce His Kingdom. What is the first requirement for entry into the Kingdom? Repentance!

When Jesus started His ministry, He paid John the Baptist the greatest compliment possible: He took up exactly where John left off.

> From that time Jesus began to preach and to say, "Repent, for the kingdom of heaven is at hand."
>
> Matthew 4:17

To *repent* means: I lay down my rebellion. I do not set my own standards, do my own thing or think my own way. I turn my back on all that and submit without reservation to God's righteous Ruler, who is Jesus.

Believe

After repentance comes faith. Many people struggling for faith cannot believe because they have never repented. There is no genuine scriptural faith for salvation apart from repentance.

So turn your back on the rebel system, come into the Kingdom and submit to the King! That is true repentance. And that way lies deliverance from the system of the world.

Questions for the Study

1. What is meant by the term *the world*?
2. What is the dividing line between those who are in the world and those who are in the Kingdom of God?
3. What are the three basic categories of temptations?
4. What are some of the characteristics of the world of which we need to be aware?
5. What is the way out of the world's system?

Part 4

HOW TO APPROPRIATE WHAT GOD HAS PROVIDED

16

FROM LEGAL TO EXPERIENTIAL

In the final three chapters I will give practical instruction on how you can appropriate all that God has provided through the atonement. First, though, I will recapitulate the two main subjects we have covered so far.

First, I analyzed the nine aspects of the exchange that took place when Jesus died on the cross:

1. Jesus was punished that I might be forgiven.
2. Jesus was wounded that I might be healed.
3. Jesus was made sin with my sinfulness that I might be made righteous with His righteousness.
4. Jesus died my death that I might share His life.
5. Jesus was made a curse that I might receive the blessing.
6. Jesus endured my poverty that I might share His abundance.
7. Jesus bore my shame that I might share His glory.
8. Jesus endured my rejection that I might have His acceptance.
9. My old man was crucified in Him that the new man might come to life in me.

I encourage you to commit these exchanges to memory. They are the vital transactions of the cross that should define and shape our very lives.

Then we looked at five different aspects of deliverance through the application of the cross in our lives, all contained in Galatians. Through the cross we receive:

1. Deliverance from this present evil age
2. Deliverance from the law
3. Deliverance from self
4. Deliverance from the flesh
5. Deliverance from the world

All this is what God has done. But it does us no good unless we know how to appropriate it. That is my theme for the balance of this book.

Let me add that if you miss what God has provided, it will not be because it is too difficult, but because it is too simple! There is nothing complicated in God's plan for appropriating His salvation.

The Pattern from Joshua

The book of Joshua contains a wonderful pattern for us to follow. Joshua had been given the tremendous responsibility of bringing the Israelites into the land of Canaan after the death of Moses—and Moses was a hard act to follow. Here is what the Lord said to Joshua:

"Moses My servant is dead. Now therefore, arise, go over this Jordan, you and all this people, to the land which I am giving to them—the children of Israel. Every place that

the sole of your foot will tread upon I have given you, as
I said to Moses."

Joshua 1:2–3

God's promise employs two different tenses. In verse 2 He
said, "I am giving." In verse 3 He said, "I have given."
We know the Lord is the disposer of everything in heaven
and earth: "The earth is the LORD's, and all its fullness" (Psalm
24:1). When the Lord gives something, that settles it; there
is no arguing about it. In this case the Lord said, "*I am giving* you this territory that you see in front of you." Then He
said, "*I have given* it to you." From that moment on, legally,
the entire land of Canaan belonged to the sons of Israel. Experientially, however, they did not actually occupy anything
more than they had before the Lord spoke.

The children of Israel could have had two wrong reactions.
The first would have been discouragement: "The Lord said
He gave it all to us, but we have nothing more than we had
before!"

The other reaction would have been presumption—the
very opposite of discouragement. They could have lined up
on the east bank of the Jordan, folded their arms, looked
westward and said, "It's all ours." Yet still they would have
had no more than before they started.

Or they could have been a little more adventurous. They
could have crossed the Jordan, lined up on the west bank,
looked westward, folded their arms and *then* said, "It's all
ours." Legally they would have been right. Experientially they
would have been wrong. The Canaanites still knew who actually possessed the land.

The Application for the Church

Sometimes the Church can be like that. Whichever side of the Jordan we happen to be on, we may look across at the Promised Land and say, "It's all ours." Legally we are right, but experientially we are wrong. I have heard people say, "I got it all when I was saved." My answer to that is, "If you got it all, where is it all? Let's see it."

But it is perfectly true. Legally, once we are born again, we are heirs of God and joint heirs with Jesus Christ. Everything that belongs to Jesus belongs to us. We do not yet possess it, however, since there is a distinction between the legal and the experiential.

Legally everything Jesus did on the cross is already ours. It has been provided. But experientially we have not entered into everything He has provided. I doubt that anyone has appropriated in experience all that Jesus provided through His death on the cross.

Remember one of the Scriptures we looked at in chapter 1: "By one offering He has perfected forever those who are being sanctified" (Hebrews 10:14). The cross is the one offering. God is saying, "I have given it." But being sanctified is like crossing the river. We must march into the land and take possession of it.

Fighting for What We Get

God performed two tremendous miracles to bring the Israelites into the Promised Land: the heaping up of the Jordan River, as the people crossed, and the destruction of Jericho. But from that time on, they had to fight for everything they got. This is true in the Christian life, as well. God will do certain miracles to bring you in. After that, you get only what you fight for, and if you do not fight for it, you do not obtain it!

Historically the Israelites did not take over the whole land at that time. They coexisted with the alien peoples—which was a disaster for them. This, too, is a picture of the Church, trying to move in and coexist with enemy forces that should not be there.

Joshua and the Israelites entering into their inheritance is a pattern for you and me. Do not fold your arms and say, "It's all ours." You are bound to be disappointed. And do not be discouraged if you find yourself involved in tremendous battles. It is part of the process.

Being Restored to Our Inheritance

A relevant passage in Obadiah, one of the shortest of all the prophetic books, delivers a powerful message about being restored to our inheritance. Verse 17 pictures the restoration of Israel at the close of this age. It is underway at present, although it has much farther to go.

On Mount Zion there shall be deliverance, and there shall be holiness; the house of Jacob shall possess their possessions.

Obadiah 17

Notice three crucial ideas: *deliverance, holiness* and *God's people possessing their possessions.* (It is possible to have possessions that we never possess.) These are the steps, according to a very simple outline, by which God's people will be restored to their inheritance.

I am intimately involved in Israel and the Middle East, though I am not Jewish. My view of history is that the Jews, because of disobedience, have been exiled for something like nineteen centuries from their God-given inheritance. At present they are on their way back.

This is true not only of Israel but of God's other covenant people, the Church. For almost the same period of time, the Church has been exiled from her God-given inheritance in Christ. If you compare the Church portrayed in the book of Acts with the Church down through the centuries, you would have to agree there is little correspondence between them. Israel returning to her geographical inheritance, then, is a pattern and challenge for the Church returning to her spiritual inheritance in Christ. The steps are the same: *deliverance, holiness, possessing our possessions.*

In the previous section, and again at the beginning of this chapter, we looked at the five forms of deliverance identified in the book of Galatians. These deliverances are essential if God's people are to regain their inheritance.

Nor will we claim our inheritance without holiness. Remember Hebrews 10:14:

> By one offering He has perfected forever those who are being sanctified [or made holy].

As we progress in holiness, in other words, we are moving back into our inheritance.

Where Does Faith Come In?

Now we come to the practical aspect: How can we appropriate the provision made for us by the cross?

The first thing we have to emphasize is faith:

> Without faith it is impossible to please Him, for he who comes to God must believe that He is, and that He is a rewarder of those who diligently seek Him.
>
> Hebrews 11:6

It is no use trying to please God without faith; that is impossible. What must we believe? According to Hebrews 11:6, we must believe two things concerning God: "that He is, and that He is a rewarder of those who diligently seek Him." Most people believe God exists. That is not enough. You must believe that if you seek God diligently, He will reward you. Faith is essential, but something else is essential, too: *diligence*.

Examine the Bible carefully and see if you can find anything in it that speaks well of laziness. It does not have one good word to say for laziness! The Bible condemns drunkenness, but it condemns laziness far more severely. Some of our values in the Church are distorted, however, because we condemn people who are drunk and tolerate people who are lazy.

Not only is faith necessary, but diligence is also essential. God has no rewards for laziness. This requires adjusted priorities! We need to have faith that if we seek God *diligently*, we will be rewarded.

There will be times when you believe that you are seeking God diligently, yet you seem to get no reward. (I am sure I am not the only person to whom this has happened!) This is when you must hold on in faith. Hebrews says God rewards those who seek Him diligently. Whether you see it or feel it, whatever happens, your reward is sure. It may not come when you expect it. It may not come the way you expect it. But it is sure. God rewards "those who diligently seek Him."

How do we get such faith?

Early on I described how I lay sick for a whole year in the hospital, seeking faith desperately—and then God gave me a wonderful Scripture. How I thank God for Romans 10:17! It was a ray of light in my darkness:

Faith comes by hearing, and hearing by the word of God.

This Scripture was my lifeline out of the hospital. It is still very real to me.

But let's not oversimplify it. Some people say faith comes by hearing the Word of God, but that is not exactly what Paul says. He says that what comes from the Word of God is hearing, and what comes from hearing is faith. These are two stages. When you expose yourself to the Word of God with an open heart and mind, what first comes is hearing—the ability to hear what God is saying. It becomes real to you. And then out of hearing develops faith.

Give God Time

The problem is, many of us do not allow the time needed for hearing to produce faith. You have to expose yourself to the Word of God without setting time limits. That is one thing I have discovered in my walk with the Lord—not to set time limits for God. If we begin to pray knowing we have only half an hour, we will receive only what we can get in half an hour. If we have the attitude, on the other hand, that we are here to hear from God with no time limits, it is different.

God does not offer instant faith. We are so used to instant everything that we assume God deals that way, too. Many in the Church think God is some kind of heavenly vending machine. Find the right coin, put it in the right slot and get the right soft drink. God is not like that. He is not a machine; He is a Person. You have to relate to Him in a very personal way to get the results.

So I suggest you prepare to give more time than most Christians presently give to hearing what God is saying to you through His Word. If you do not take time for hearing, all you will do is read the Bible. Faith does not come by reading the Bible; it comes by hearing from God *through* the Bible. Hearing first, then faith.

Let God Speak to You

In Romans 10:17 the Greek for "word" is *rhema*. It refers not to the Word of God established forever in heaven (for which the Greek word is *logos*), but to the word God is speaking to you at any given moment. As Jesus said in Matthew 4:4, *"Man shall not live by bread alone, but by every word* [rhema] *that proceeds from the mouth of God."*

We do not live by a printed volume called the Bible, if I can put it that way; we live by the Word made real to us personally at any moment by the Holy Spirit. The Bible consists of white sheets of paper with black marks on them. Those black marks do us no good. What transforms them into something that produces faith is the Holy Spirit, who makes the Word of God a living word. It then becomes a *rhema*.

During those first months in the British Army when I was studying the Bible as a philosopher, I felt it was my duty to know what the Bible had to say. There was nothing in it that attracted me; I simply felt I could not speak with authority about the Bible if I did not know what it said. Reading the Bible was wearisome! Only determination kept me going.

No book is going to beat me, I thought. *I'll start at the beginning and read it through to the end.*

Then, after nine months, I had a supernatural encounter with Jesus in the middle of the night. It was not an intellectual decision but an experience. The next day, when I picked up the Bible, it was totally different! It was just as if there were only two persons in the universe—God and I. The Bible was now the voice of God speaking to me personally. It was dramatic!

This is where each of us has to come. Whatever it takes, don't stop short of a relationship with God in which His Word speaks to you personally. First you need to cultivate hearing. Then out of that comes faith!

How to Read the Bible

May I offer two suggestions on how to approach the Scriptures?

As God's Word

Paul expressed pride in the Thessalonian Christians, telling them they were an example to all the other Christians around. He stated one reason for their success in 1 Thessalonians 2:13:

> When you received the word of God which you heard from us, you welcomed it not as the word of men, but as it is in truth, the word of God, which also effectively works in you who believe.

When you receive Scripture not as the word of men—not on the same level with human writings and human wisdom, but as God Himself speaking to you—it will do its work in you. When you open your heart by faith to God's Word, it will do in you what God has said it will do. It "effectively works in you who believe."

With Meekness

A second requirement is found in the epistle of James:

Lay aside all filthiness and overflow of wickedness, and receive with meekness the implanted word, which is able to save your souls.

James 1:21

What does it mean to receive God's Word with meekness? It means acknowledging that God is the teacher and we are the pupils. We do not tell God how He should run the universe, nor how He should manage our lives. With humility we let Him teach us.

Just recently I came up with a new definition of faith, a very simple one: *Faith is taking God seriously.* Reading the Bible with faith is taking seriously everything God says. When God says, "Do this," we do it.

Here is an example. If you catch on to this, it will change your life!

First Thessalonians 5:18 says, "In everything give thanks." In how many things? In everything. Do you believe that? Do you take it seriously? Do you do it?

When you put on your clothes, thank God for your clothes. Bear in mind that many do not have enough to wear. What do you do when you put your shoes on? Many in the world do not have shoes. When you get into the car, thank God for your car. When you drive along the highway, thank God for the highway.

Even if it is jammed with cars, it took a lot of money and labor to build that road. Do not take it for granted.

In other words, do not just thank God sporadically when it comes to your mind, but make it a habit to thank Him in everything. It will transform you!

This is an example of what I mean by receiving with meekness the Word of God. You may be saying, "That doesn't sound reasonable to me. After all, I paid for my clothes and my shoes and my car." No, receive His Word with meekness. Say, "Okay, Lord, Your Word says to thank You, so I *will* thank You for all these things."

Moving from Legal to Experiential

I close this chapter with a summary on how to move from the legal to the experiential through applying God's Word. Jesus said:

"Seek first the kingdom of God and His righteousness."

Matthew 6:33

Give God and His Word priority in your life over everything else. Seek God and His Word first. Remember to spend enough time in the Word to really build your faith. Receive Scripture as God's personal word to you. And receive His Word with meekness, duly obeying its commands.

Let these things take priority over everything else in your life. When your priorities are adjusted and you have the attitude toward God and His Word that permits faith to come in, you are on your way to receiving what God has provided for you. Then you can appropriate all that Jesus provided through His death on the cross.

Questions for the Study

1. What is the difference between *legal* and *experiential*?
2. According to Obadiah 17, how can we be restored to our inheritance?
3. What are some practical steps we can take to appropriate the provision made by the cross?
4. What do we need to do to start moving from the legal to the experiential?

17

OUR PERSONAL GUIDE TO ALL-INCLUSIVE SALVATION

We have seen that the sacrifice of Jesus on the cross provided everything that will ever be needed, for time and eternity, for every believer. It is complete, but our appropriation of it is progressive. How do we enter into all that God has provided through the sacrifice of Jesus on the cross?

In the previous chapter I pointed out the first essential requirement: faith. The person who comes to God must believe. Faith is not an option. According to Hebrews 11:6 you must believe that God exists and that He rewards those who seek Him diligently.

In this chapter we see another requirement: learning to relate to the Holy Spirit. The Spirit guides us to appropriate all the provisions of Christ's atonement. He personally will lead you to what you need.

Salvation is not just getting your sins forgiven—although, thank God, that is an essential part of it! Salvation is the total provision of God for His people through the sacrifice of Jesus.

In chapter 4 I spoke about the Greek word *sozo*, normally translated "save." I pointed out that the word *sozo* is used in the gospels for healing the sick, delivering people from evil spirits, raising the dead and the total preservation of God's people. This one word describes all these benefits. My definition of *salvation*, then, is that it covers everything provided for us—spiritual, physical, emotional, material—by the sacrifice of Jesus on the cross, for time and for eternity.

Being born again is a one-time experience. It happens once and brings you into salvation. Being saved is a progressive experience—something you have to walk out, explore and possess. Salvation is like the land of Canaan, which Israel was required to conquer in stages.

In Psalm 78 we find that salvation covers everything God did for His people from Egypt to the Promised Land. It includes every act of mercy and blessing and provision. It covers their deliverance out of Egypt, their passage through the Red Sea, the coming of the cloud upon them, the provision of manna, the supply of water from the rock, the facts that their clothes and shoes never wore out and that He drove out the nations before them. All this and more is summed up in that one word *salvation*.

But Israel was unbelieving and disobedient and "spoke against God" (verse 19).

The LORD heard this and was furious; so a fire was kindled against Jacob, and anger also came up against Israel, because they did not believe in God, *and did not trust in His salvation.*

verses 21–22, emphasis added

What was the Israelites' basic problem? They did not believe in God or trust in His full salvation. It is apparent from this passage that unbelief makes God angry. Could it be that the same problem is often true of the Church? We do not believe in God as He wants us to believe. We do not trust in His complete provision for every need. Yet God wants us to trust Him for everything.

In Romans 8:32 God declares that His provision for us includes "all things." This verse is like a blank check. God has signed the check and put your name on it, but He has not written in the amount. You write in whatever you need!

He who did not spare His own Son, but delivered Him up for us all, how shall He not with Him also freely give us *all things?*

emphasis added

If God was willing to give Jesus to die on the cross—the most precious treasure in the universe, the possession closest to God's own heart—there can be nothing else that He will withhold. Bear in mind that without Jesus you have no claim on anything from God except judgment. But with Him and because of Him, God will give you all you need. There is nothing more to be done; there is no extra charge. *God gives you all things freely.*

That is all-inclusive salvation. It comes through the gift of the sacrifice of Jesus on the cross. But we cannot enter into this full salvation until we recognize the part that the Holy Spirit plays.

What Does the Holy Spirit Do?

The Greek language uses three genders—masculine, feminine and neuter. The Greek word for Spirit is *pneuma*—wind, breath or spirit—and it is neuter. The correct pronoun to substitute for *Spirit*, therefore, would be *it*. But when Jesus spoke about the Holy Spirit—in John 16:13, for example— He did not say *it*; He said *He*: "When *He*, the Spirit of truth, has come."

Thus the laws of grammar are broken in this passage. Jesus is emphasizing that in spite of normal grammatical usage, the Holy Spirit is not an *it* but a *He*. The Holy Spirit is as much a Person as God the Father and God the Son.

One of the keys to success in the Christian life is learning to relate to the Holy Spirit as a Person. If we invite Him in and fulfill the conditions, the Holy Spirit will come to us as a Person. We must learn to relate to Him as a Person. Make friends with Him; He is a good Person to be friendly with!

What does the Holy Spirit do to help us appropriate all the provisions of Christ's atonement?

He Administrates Salvation

The Holy Spirit is the sole Administrator of salvation. He holds the key to the storehouse of all God's provisions. He opens the treasure house of God and gives us what we need. Yet He is one of the most neglected persons in the Church! Even Pentecostals and charismatics, who talk a lot about the Holy Spirit, often ignore Him.

If you want to receive your inheritance and get what God has provided, make friends with the Holy Spirit. In John 16 Jesus was getting ready to leave His disciples and was preparing them for what was to come.

> "I tell you the truth. It is to your advantage that I go away; for if I do not go away, the Helper [the Holy Spirit] will not come to you; but if I depart, I will send Him to you."
>
> verse 7

Notice that Jesus was talking about an exchange of persons. "I as a Person am going back to heaven," He was saying, "but in My place I will send another Person." Then He said something amazing: "It is to your advantage that I go. In other words, you'll be better off with Me in heaven and the Holy Spirit on earth, than you are now with Me on earth and the Holy Spirit in heaven."

Most Christians do not see this. We think how wonderful it would be to have lived back in the days when Jesus was on earth with His disciples. It *would* be wonderful, but Jesus was saying, "That was just a transitional stage. Now it is to your advantage that I leave you and the Holy Spirit takes My place on earth. Then from heaven I will be able to work through the Spirit everywhere on earth at the same time, without being limited to a physical body. So it is to your advantage that I leave you."

He Guides Us into Truth and Points to Jesus

Jesus goes on to say:

> "When He, the Spirit of truth, has come, He will guide you into all truth; for He will not speak on His own authority

[I prefer *He will not speak from Himself*], but whatever He hears He will speak; and He will tell you things to come."

John 16:13

The Holy Spirit is the Person in the universe who least attracts attention to Himself. That is why, in a sense, we tend to ignore Him. Jesus said that when the Holy Spirit comes, He says nothing from Himself, but only what He hears the Father and Son say. To whom does the Holy Spirit draw attention? To Jesus, who said, "He will glorify Me" (John 16:14).

One of the great tests of whether something is from the Holy Spirit is not the amount of noise it produces, but whether it glorifies Jesus. If it exalts a human personality or focuses on a doctrine or denomination, it is not the work of the Holy Spirit. The Holy Spirit does not glorify those things. Rather, He glorifies Jesus.

If we want to attract the Holy Spirit—an activity well worth engaging in!—we should take time to praise and lift up the name of Jesus. Then the Holy Spirit will say to Himself, *Now that's what I like to hear. I'll go and spend some time with those people.*

It is worthwhile learning what the Holy Spirit likes and meeting His requirements.

He Helps Us Discern Truth

Not only will the Holy Spirit guide us into all truth, but He is the only reliable Guide. John wrote to the early Christians, "You have an anointing from the Holy One, and you know all things" (1 John 2:20). John was referring to the Holy Spirit. Would that God's people today had that anointing to discern between what is true and what is false! Often "Spirit-filled" Christians are the easiest people on earth to fool. They have not learned to distinguish between the noisy, the fleshly, the ostentatious and that which glorifies Jesus.

Look at John 16:14–15:

> "[The Spirit] will glorify Me, for He will take of what is Mine and declare it to you. All things that the Father has are Mine. Therefore I said that He will take of Mine and declare it to you."

Notice the modesty of Jesus! He does not want to leave us with the impression that He is the original owner of anything. He says, "It is Mine only because the Father gave it to Me." What a beautiful example of glorifying another! The Holy Spirit glorifies Jesus, and Jesus glorifies the Father. Then He points us to the Holy Spirit. He says, "When the Holy Spirit comes, He will take of what is Mine and declare or reveal or impart it to you."

So we see that the Holy Spirit holds the key to the storehouse of the treasures of God. All that the Father and the Son have is administered by the Holy Spirit. Many Christians study doctrine, but they have never made friends with the Holy Spirit. But it really is worth making friends with Him!

A Biblical Picture

We in the Church have a wonderful Guide and Protector on our long journey through life: the Holy Spirit. Genesis 24 gives a beautiful picture of His role, in the story of Abraham finding a bride for his son Isaac.

"I will not take a bride for my son from the daughters of Canaan," Abraham says, reflecting a typical Middle Eastern practice to this day. "She must be from my own clan." So the patriarch sends his steward to his own people to find the right girl and bring her back.

In this story Abraham is a type of God the Father. Isaac, the only begotten son, is a type of Jesus Christ. Rebekah, the chosen bride, is a type of the Church. One more character, the servant, who is never named, is a type of the Holy Spirit. Genesis 24 is the Holy Spirit's self-portrait, but He never signs it.

That unnamed servant sets out with ten camels laden with gifts. (If you have spent any time in the Middle East, as I have, you realize how much a camel can carry!) Similarly, when the Holy Spirit comes, He does not come empty-handed. He has ten camels with Him, laden with gifts. (You really are foolish if you do not make friends with Him!)

When the servant comes to the well in search of the right girl, he prays, "God of my master Abraham, I ask that the right one will offer water not only for me"—which anyone would give—"but for my camels, too."

Since a camel can drink forty gallons of water, and the servant has ten camels, that young woman would be pumping up to four hundred gallons of water. Any girl who would do that is not just kind and pretty, but she has muscle. What a wife she would make!

This always reminds me of a comment from a young man in Africa, where for five years I trained students to become teachers. I would walk around with my students and ask them questions without warning. Once I asked this young man, "Tell me, what kind of girl do you want to marry?" Without breaking stride he answered, "She must be brown and muscu-

lar." I don't know exactly what color Rebekah was, but I guarantee she was not white, and she certainly was muscular!

While the servant is standing by the well, along comes a
young woman, to whom the servant says, "Give me water,
please," and she says, "Drink, and I'll give your camels a drink,
too."

That is a picture of the Church!—not a delicate young lady
who sits in the front seat and sings hymns, but a woman with
muscles prepared to work and to lay down her life.

The servant says to himself, *This is the girl.*

After the servant meets Rebekah's family and tells them
of Abraham's desire to find a wife for his son, they put the
question to Rebekah: "Will you go with this man?"

Deciding her destiny, she says, "I will go."

That is faith. She has known the servant less than 24
hours, but she sets out on a long, dangerous journey with
him as her sole guide and protector. We, too, as the Church,
have a long and dangerous journey before we meet our
Bridegroom, but we have a wonderful Guide and Protector, the Holy Spirit.

Furthermore, Rebekah has never seen the man she is
going to marry. All she knows about Isaac, she has learned
from the servant. All we will ever know about Jesus, until
we meet Him, we learn from the Holy Spirit. We will miss
a lot if we do not cultivate a deep, intimate relationship
with the Spirit.

Rely on the Spirit for Ministry

Romans 8:14, which we have looked at already, is an important passage for those who desire to prepare themselves
for ministry in the Body of Christ:

As many as are led by the Spirit of God, these are sons of God.

Paul uses the continuing present tense: as many as are *regularly led* by the Spirit of God. Who are God's sons? Those who are led *regularly* by the Spirit. In other words, I am living as a son of God when I am being led regularly by His Spirit.

You, too, need to be led not by rules, principles, techniques, procedures and all the rest, but by God's Spirit. You may have learned various rules or principles or procedures or techniques, and I am not saying those are wrong. But it *is* wrong to rely on them completely. There is only one Person we can rely on completely: the Holy Spirit. If we rely on Him, He will guide us to any rule, principle, procedure or technique that is appropriate. But if we rely solely on the rules, we will get only what human resources have to offer.

As Christians we should be able to offer the world more than that. For example, a professional psychologist has his rules and comes up with a diagnosis that may or may not be right. But we are called to do more than that. We have a wonderful Friend whose name is the Holy Spirit. He places divine, supernatural resources at our disposal.

Please don't become an amateur psychiatrist! Psychiatrists can be dangerous, but amateur psychiatrists can be extremely dangerous. When someone comes to you for counseling, don't go immediately down a list of symptoms. Rely on the Holy Spirit. He may guide you to the list of symptoms, and the list may be right—yet you cannot rely on it. You can rely only on the Spirit Himself.

Some people use the counseling technique of taking you all the way back from your present age to childhood, infancy and then to the womb. But when Jesus encountered the Samaritan woman at the well, He did not take her all the way back to childhood and infancy; He had a word of knowledge from the Holy Spirit: "You have had five husbands, and the one whom you now have is not your husband" (John 4:18). Jesus did not need to say anything more; that insight exposed her whole heart and life to Him instantly.

My first wife, Lydia, who is with the Lord, was a very unusual lady by any standard. She was Danish, and she was a real Viking!

Once, when we were contemplating buying a house, two hard-boiled real estate women came to tell us about the house they wanted us to buy. They were determined to sell.

As they sat together on the sofa, Lydia looked at one of them and said suddenly, "I think your legs are unequal. Would you like my husband to pray for you?"

How could she say no? So I knelt in front of the realtor, discovered her legs were, indeed, of unequal lengths and prayed for her. The short leg grew out before our eyes. She was in a state of shock.

I moved quickly over to the next woman.

"May I check your legs?"

They grew out, too.

Then I said, "What about your arms?"

"Oh, no," she said. "That's enough!"

But from that time onward those women were different persons. Instead of hard-boiled realtors, they became real people with real problems that they wanted to share with Lydia and me. And they sold us a fine house!

Who made the difference? The Holy Spirit.

The Holy Spirit will lead you to appropriate all the promises of Christ's atonement. He holds the key to the storehouse of all God's provisions. And He will be your personal Guide.

Questions for the Study

1. What one word describes all the benefits we receive by the sacrifice of Jesus on the cross?
2. Is there anything, according to Romans 8:32, that God withholds from us?
3. What part does the Holy Spirit play in our entering into full salvation?
4. Who holds the key to the storehouse of God's provision, and what is our relationship with that Person?

18

POSSESSING OUR
POSSESSIONS

In the previous chapters we saw that through the sacrifice of Jesus on the cross, God has provided for us a complete and perfect salvation, "perfect in every respect, perfect in every aspect." God has also made available to us a divine Guide to lead us into our inheritance. That Guide is the Holy Spirit.

We looked at the experience of Joshua and the children of Israel as a pattern of how God brought His people into their inheritance. In Joshua 1:2 God said, "I am giving" the land. Then in verse 3 God said, "I have given" the land. From then on, legally, the land belonged to the Israelites, even though they had not yet begun to occupy it. What was legally theirs had to become theirs in experience.

Exactly the same is true for us, in respect to the sacrifice of Jesus on the cross. Jesus has done it all. He has provided a salvation that is perfect, complete and all-inclusive. But we have to move from the legal to the experiential; the cross has to become real in our lives. We have to appropriate in reality the full provision that Jesus has made for us. This is not a single experience but a progressive series of experiences.

We also looked at various uses in the New Testament of the word *salvation*. We saw that it includes a number of different ways that Jesus works in our lives. His salvation is not confined merely to the forgiveness of sin. It also includes physical healing, deliverance from demons, even raising a person from the dead. All this and more is included in the one comprehensive word *salvation*.

All this has been made available to us. Legally it is already ours through faith in Christ. But like Joshua and the Israelites we have to pass from the legal to the experiential. The basic scriptural pattern by which we do this was established on the Day of Pentecost, as recorded in Acts 2:38–39.

After Peter had described the life, death and resurrection of Jesus, the convicted but still unconverted multitude cried out, "Men and brethren, what shall we do?" (verse 37). In response, Peter, as the spokesman of God and of the Church, stated three successive requirements: *Repent, be baptized, receive the Holy Spirit.* These are the three scriptural steps through which we may enter into the full salvation that Jesus has obtained for us. We will briefly consider, in turn, what is contained in each of these.

1. Repent

For a full understanding of repentance, we need to examine the different words used in the Greek of the New Testament and in the Hebrew of the Old Testament. The Greek verb *metanoo* means "to change your mind." Essentially it is a *de-*

cision. The Hebrew word *shub* means "to turn back" or "to turn around." It is an *action*.

When we combine these two words, we get a complete picture of repentance. It is a *decision* followed by an *action*. First I make a decision. Then I follow it up with the appropriate action.

A vivid example of this is provided by the parable of the Prodigal Son in Luke 15:11–32. First he made a decision: "I will arise and go to my father" (verse 18). Then he followed it up by the appropriate action: He turned around and went back home by the way he had come.

Alternatively, to use a contemporary example, repentance is making a U-turn. You have been traveling in the wrong direction. You stop, make a 180-degree turn and begin to travel in the opposite direction. Your repentance is not complete until you actually begin to travel in the new direction.

God's requirement of repentance was stated first by the forerunner of Jesus, John the Baptist, in Matthew 3:2: "Repent, for the kingdom of heaven is at hand!" It was reiterated by Jesus Himself in Mark 1:15: "The kingdom of God is at hand. Repent, and believe in the gospel."

Unfortunately a great deal of preaching today almost completely omits this first step we need to take: *repent*.

A few years ago I was assisting in a big meeting in Southeast Asia. Most of the people were from a Chinese background; very few were familiar with the Bible. The preacher gave some good teaching on how to be healed through the Word of God, but he did not use the word *repent*. Then he said, "If you want healing, come forward and pray."

I found myself trying to minister to some of the scores of people who surged to the front. Their backgrounds included ancestor worship, occult practices and idolatry, and they wanted Jesus on top of all that! But Jesus will never agree to being an add-on to many other things in our lives. He is the unique foundation of all Christian belief or He is nothing.

The preacher should have said, "Turn from the occult and from your wicked ways. Give up your ancestor worship and the idolatrous practices you have lived with for generations. Make a clean break and come to Jesus." But unfortunately repentance was not part of his message. The result of that meeting was confusion rather than effective ministry. Few people, if any, got saved, because they had not met the first requirement for salvation: repentance.

Many churches today are propagating a message something like this: "If you want to be free of all your problems, just come and receive Jesus." But receiving Jesus does not resolve all your problems. In fact, initially you may encounter a whole new set of problems!

The unvarying first requirement for salvation is repentance. The New Testament acknowledges no such thing as believing for salvation without repenting. It always puts repenting before believing. In Luke 24:46–47 the resurrected Christ explains to His disciples the necessity of His death:

> "Thus it is written, and thus it was necessary for the Christ [Messiah] to suffer and to rise from the dead the third day, and that repentance and remission [forgiveness] of sins should be preached in His name to all nations, beginning at Jerusalem."

What was the message of the Gospel that Jesus committed to His disciples? Not just the forgiveness of sins, but repentance first, and then the forgiveness of sins.

Later, in Acts 20:20–21, as Paul is describing his ministry in Ephesus, he says:

"I kept back nothing that was helpful, but proclaimed it to you, and taught you publicly and from house to house, testifying to Jews, and also to Greeks, repentance toward God and faith toward our Lord Jesus Christ."

Paul outlines very simply the message he preached to everyone, Jew or Greek, in public or in private: Repent and have faith toward God.

At the close of the New Testament, in Revelation 2–3, John records the message of Jesus to seven churches in the province of Asia. To five of them His first requirement was to *repent*. Almost certainly the proportion of churches today needing to repent would be no less.

Over the years I have counseled Christians with various kinds of problems. On thinking back over all that I heard, I concluded that in most cases there was one root problem: *the failure to repent.* Had these people received and obeyed the message of repentance, in most cases they would have had no further need for counseling. Their problems would have dissolved.

In our unredeemed condition, the primary sin of which we all need to repent is *rebellion against God.* At the end of World War II, the Allies communicated to the Axis powers the condition on which they would make peace: *unconditional surrender.* They would make peace on no other basis. God lays down the same terms. He will not make peace on any other basis than unconditional surrender. No arguments, no demands, no excuses, no reservations. Our unequivocal response must be, "Here I am, God. I submit! Tell me what to do."

Turning from sin, submitting yourself to God and committing yourself to the Lordship of Jesus is true repentance. Throughout Scripture it is the primary, non-negotiable requirement for salvation.

2. Be Baptized

The verb *baptize* is directly derived from a Greek word that means "to dip" or "to immerse" beneath the surface of water or some other fluid. As a religious ordinance, the Jewish people in the time of Jesus already practiced certain ceremonies, which included baptism. Baptism also played a central role in the ministry of John the Baptist. When people responded to his message of repentance, he required them to be baptized in the River Jordan. John's baptism was, therefore, a public acknowledgment that a person had repented of his sins, but it went no further than that.

Jesus Himself submitted to John's baptism as He began His own ministry. But the baptism of Jesus was not an acknowledgment or confession of sin, because Jesus had committed no sin. In Matthew 3:15 Jesus explained the reason He was baptized: "to fulfill all righteousness." By His submission to the baptism of John, Jesus fulfilled, or completed, by an outward act, the inner righteousness that He possessed eternally. It was the doorway through which He entered His own public ministry.

The ministry of John the Baptist, however, was transitional. It sealed up the ministry of the Old Testament prophets and opened the way for the ministry of Jesus and of the Gospel. Once Jesus had completed His earthly ministry and paid the price for our sins, the baptism of John was no longer valid. Acts 19:1–5 records how Paul encountered in Ephesus certain disciples of John the Baptist and explained to them the full message of the Gospel, centering on the death and resurrection of Jesus. Afterward these disciples of John were baptized with Christian baptism in the name of the Lord Jesus.

The distinctive feature of Christian baptism is that it is an act by which the person being baptized publicly identifies himself with Jesus in His death, burial and resurrection. Paul reminded the Colossians that they were "buried with [Christ] in baptism, in which you also were raised with Him through faith in the working of God, who raised Him from the dead" (Colossians 2:12). In fulfillment of God's purpose through the Gospel, all those who claimed salvation through faith in the atonement of Jesus were required to give a public testimony to this by the act of baptism. This was a distinctive sign that they were committing themselves to Jesus as His disciples.

In non-Christian communities around the world, such as Muslim or Hindu communities, the public act of baptism marks a person out as a disciple of Jesus, and it often provokes strong reactions from the unbelievers.

In Mark 16:15–16 Jesus sent out His first apostles with this instruction:

"Go into all the world and preach the gospel to every creature. He who believes and is baptized will be saved; but he who does not believe will be condemned."

Christian baptism is not an addendum to the process of salvation; it is the consummation of that process. Jesus has not promised salvation to those who believe without being baptized, and there is no record in the New Testament of any person who claimed salvation through faith in Christ without being baptized.

The final emphasis in Christian baptism, however, is not on death or burial, but on resurrection, which opens the door to a totally new style of living. This is beautifully summed up by Paul in Colossians 3:1–4:

> If then you were raised with Christ, seek those things which are above, where Christ is, sitting at the right hand of God. Set your mind on things above, not on things on the earth. For you died, and your life is hidden with Christ in God. When Christ who is our life appears, then you also will appear with Him in glory.

3. Receive the Holy Spirit

This is the third and culminating step of the process by which we enter our inheritance in Christ. For a proper understanding of what is involved, we need to recognize that the New Testament speaks of two different ways to receive the Holy Spirit.

John 20:21–22 records that Jesus after His resurrection first appeared to His disciples in a group:

> Jesus said to them again, "Peace to you! As the Father has sent Me, I also send you." And when He had said this, He breathed on them, and said to them, "Receive the Holy Spirit."

More literally verse 22 could be rendered, "He breathed _into_ them, and said to them, 'Receive Holy Breath.'" His action was suited to His words. At that moment the disciples received from Jesus the Holy Spirit as divine Breath. They were, in fact, born again of the Holy Spirit. They received divine resurrection life—life that had triumphed over Satan, sin, death and the grave.

It is in the light of this that the apostle says in 1 John 5:4: "Whatever is born of God overcomes the world." There is no power in the universe that can defeat the divine, eternal life of God received by every believer in Jesus who is born again of the Spirit.

But the disciples still had more to receive of the Holy Spirit. In the forty-day period between the resurrection and ascension of Jesus,

> He commanded them not to depart from Jerusalem, but to wait for the Promise of the Father, "which," He said, "you have heard from Me; for John truly baptized with water, but you shall be baptized with the Holy Spirit not many days from now."
>
> Acts 1:4–5

Clearly the baptism in the Holy Spirit was something that still lay ahead for the disciples, even after their experience on Resurrection Sunday.

The fulfillment of this promise of Jesus is recorded in Acts 2:1–4:

> When the Day of Pentecost had fully come, they were all with one accord in one place. And suddenly there came a sound from heaven, as of a rushing mighty wind, and it filled the whole house where they were sitting. Then there appeared to them divided tongues, as of fire, and one sat upon each of them. And they were all filled with the Holy Spirit and began to speak with other tongues, as the Spirit gave them utterance.

There were three successive phases in the experience described above. First, there was a *baptism*, an immersion. They were all immersed in the Holy Spirit coming down over them from above. This could perhaps be described as a "Niagara Falls" baptism.

Second, there was an *infilling*. They were all individually filled with the Holy Spirit.

Third, there was an *overflow*. The Holy Spirit within them overflowed through them in supernatural speech. They glorified God in languages they had not learned and did not understand.

The experience of the disciples on the Day of Pentecost demonstrated the principle stated by Jesus in Matthew 12:34: "For out of the abundance of the heart the mouth speaks." When the heart is full, in other words, it overflows through the mouth in speech.

This experience of the Holy Spirit was the appropriate supernatural equipment to make the disciples effective as witnesses for Jesus. They were to be witnesses to events that were totally supernatural: the resurrection and ascension of Jesus. The testimony to such supernatural events required supernatural power, which was first manifested on the Day of Pentecost and continued throughout the record of the book of Acts.

This power has never been withdrawn from the Church and is still available today. In 1 Corinthians 1:4–8 Paul clearly indicates that the supernatural gifts and manifestations of the Holy Spirit are to continue in operation in the Church until the close of the age.

> I thank my God always concerning you for the grace of God which was given to you by Christ Jesus, that you were enriched in everything by Him in all utterance and all knowledge, even as the testimony of Christ was confirmed in you, *so that you come short in no gift, eagerly waiting for the revelation of our Lord Jesus Christ, who will also confirm*

*you to the end, that you may be blameless in the day of our
Lord Jesus Christ.*

emphasis added

We may sum up the operations of the Holy Spirit described
above by the following comparison between two critical days
in the record of the Church.

Resurrection Sunday	Pentecost Sunday
The resurrected Christ	The ascended Christ
The in-breathed Spirit	The outpoured Spirit
Result: Resurrection life	Result: Power to witness

For those who have received the Resurrection Sunday experience and feel their need for the Pentecost Sunday experience, Jesus offers a promise in John 7:37–39:

On the last day, that great day of the feast, Jesus stood and
cried out, saying, "If anyone thirsts, let him come to Me
and drink. He who believes in Me, as the Scripture has
said, out of his heart will flow rivers of living water." But
this He spoke concerning the Spirit, whom those believing
in Him would receive.

There are three simple requirements: Be thirsty, come to
Jesus and drink until you receive the overflow!

Old Testament Patterns

All this was vividly foreshadowed in the Old Testament
account of the deliverance of Israel out of Egypt, as Paul
describes it in 1 Corinthians 10:1–2:

All our fathers were under the cloud, all passed through the sea, all were baptized . . . in the cloud and in the sea.

First the Israelites, while still *in* Egypt, were saved from God's judgment through the blood of the Passover lamb. Throughout Scripture the sacrificial lamb represents Jesus, the Lamb of God, whose blood shed on the cross saves repentant sinners from God's judgment on their sins.

After that the Israelites were saved *out* of Egypt by what Paul describes as a double baptism. The baptism in the cloud coming down over them from above typifies the baptism of the Holy Spirit. The passing of the Israelites through the water of the Red Sea, supernaturally parted before them, typifies baptism by immersion in water. This double baptism effectively and finally separated the Israelites from Egypt—a type of this world in its fallen condition.

The baptism in the cloud is described in Exodus 14:19–20:

The Angel of God, who went before the camp of Israel, moved and went behind them; and the pillar of cloud went from before them and stood behind them. So it came between the camp of the Egyptians and the camp of Israel. Thus it was a cloud and darkness to the one [the Egyptians], and it gave light by night to the other [the Israelites], so that the one did not come near the other all that night.

In this supernatural cloud the Lord Himself came down to protect His people. It had a double effect. To the Egyptians it was dark and frightening, but to the Israelites it gave light by night. All night it kept the Egyptians from coming close to the Israelites.

It was in the cloud that the Angel of God drew near to protect His people. Jesus indicated that it was through the

Holy Spirit that He would return to make His permanent dwelling with His disciples. The cloud vividly foreshadows the outworking of the promise that Jesus gave His disciples in John 14:16–18:

> "I will pray the Father, and He will give you another Helper, that He may abide with you forever—the Spirit of truth [the Holy Spirit].... I will not leave you orphans; I will come to you."

The description of Israel's exodus from Egypt indicates that the Angel of God was in the pillar of cloud that separated the camp of Israel from the Egyptians. Likewise it is in the Holy Spirit that the Lord Jesus returns to His believing people to make His permanent dwelling with them. In this way He provides both protection and comfort for them in times of pressure.

Through this double baptism God's people began a lifetime journey that would take them to the inheritance God had prepared for them. Day by day they were guided by the same cloud that had come down over them on the shore of the Red Sea. In the daytime this cloud provided shelter from the heat of the sun, and at night it provided light in the darkness. What a wonderful type of the Holy Spirit, who is both our Guide and our Comforter!

On this journey the Israelites "all ate the same spiritual food, and all drank the same spiritual drink" (1 Corinthians 10:3–4). The food the Israelites ate was the manna that came down with the dew every morning. In Matthew 4:4, likewise, Jesus directed His disciples to the spiritual food God has prepared for His people in the present age: "Man shall not live by bread alone, but by every word that proceeds from the mouth of God." To the Christian today, spiritual strength and health come through regular, daily feeding on the Word of God that comes to us through the Scriptures.

Likewise in John 7:37–39 Jesus said:

> "If anyone thirsts, let him come to Me and drink. He who believes in Me, as the Scripture has said, out of his heart will flow rivers of living water." But this He spoke concerning the Spirit, whom those believing in Him would receive.

Every born-again Christian, indwelled by the Holy Spirit, has within himself an inexhaustible fountain of living water.

Throughout our life's journey our spiritual health and well-being depend on feeding daily on God's Word, the Scripture, and drinking daily from the fountain of the Holy Spirit within us. In my own experience as a Christian, I have learned that this comes through intimate daily fellowship with the Lord, feeding on His Word and responding to Him in prayer and worship by the prompting of the Holy Spirit within our hearts. It has also become vivid to me that the manna God provided for the Israelites on their wilderness journey had to be gathered early in the day. Otherwise, when the sun rose, its heat melted the manna. It is important for us, too, that we feed on God's Word early in the day before the heat of worldly concerns and responsibilities causes the manna to melt.

From the Red Sea onward, it was the cloud that guided the Israelites the whole of their journey through the wilderness. This vividly illustrates the words of Paul in Romans 8:14:

> As many as are led by the Spirit of God, these are the sons of God.

My aim throughout this book has been to equip and prepare you for the journey that lies ahead. The time has now come that we must part for a while. It is my heart's prayer that you will have a victorious and successful journey and that we shall meet one day face to face in our heavenly inheritance.

Questions for the Study

1. What are the three steps through which we may enter into full salvation?
2. True repentance is defined by what two words?
3. In what ways does water baptism identify us with Jesus?
4. According to Acts 2:1–4, what are the three successive phases in experiencing the baptism with the Holy Spirit?
5. Why do we need this experience with the Holy Spirit?
6. According to John 7:37–39, what are the three requirements for receiving the baptism with the Holy Spirit?
7. Throughout our life's journey, our spiritual health and well-being depend on what two things?

INDEX

Derek Prince (1915–2003) was born in India of British parents. He was educated as a scholar of Greek and Latin at Eton College and Cambridge University, England, where he held a fellowship in ancient and modern philosophy at King's College. He also studied several modern languages, including Hebrew and Aramaic, at Cambridge University and the Hebrew University in Jerusalem.

While serving with the British Army in World War II, Derek began to study the Bible and experienced a life-changing encounter with Jesus Christ. Out of that encounter he formed two conclusions: first, that Jesus Christ is alive; and second, that the Bible is a true, relevant, up-to-date book. These conclusions altered the whole course of his life, which he then devoted to studying and teaching the Bible.

Derek's main gift of explaining the Bible and its teaching in a clear, simple way has helped build a foundation of faith in millions of lives. His nondenominational, nonsectarian approach makes his teaching relevant and helpful to people from all racial and religious backgrounds.

He wrote more than fifty books, and his teaching is featured on five hundred audio and 140 video teaching messages, many of which have been translated and published in more than sixty languages. His daily radio broadcast, *Derek Prince Legacy Radio*, is translated into Arabic, Chinese (Amoy, Cantonese, Mandarin, Shanghaiese, Swatow), Croatian, German,

Malagasy, Mongolian, Russian, Samoan, Spanish and Tongan. His daily radio program continues to touch lives around the world.

For more information on Derek Prince and the many teaching resources available, please contact:

Derek Prince Ministries
P.O. Box 19501
Charlotte, NC 28219-9501
(704) 357-3556
www.derekprince.org

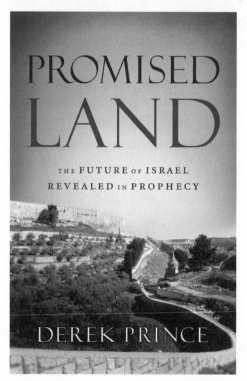

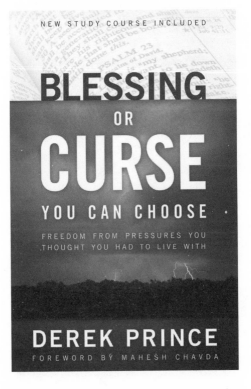

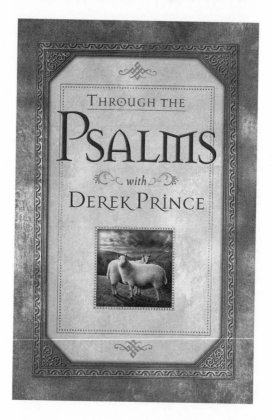